Culinary Artists
Tidewater's Regional Chefs

Andrea A. Moore

Culinary Artists: Tidewater's Regional Chefs

Culinary Art of Tidewater
P.O. Box 6231
Norfolk, VA 23508
(757) 440-0745

Cautionary Instruction: Some recipes in this book require cooking with high temperatures, open flames, grills and alcohol. Always use extreme caution and care. Never pour alcohol into a dish over an open flame or near a heat source. Author/Publisher disclaim liability for using or failure to use extreme caution and common sense when cooking with high temperatures, open flames, grills and alcohol.

Design and Photography: Kevin R. Kaiser, Virginia Beach, VA

Editors: Leah S. Wilbur and Don Laux, Fairfax, VA

Graphics: Sharon Franklin, Okra Stewdios, Portsmouth, VA

Media Consultant: Ray Horowitz, Virginia Beach, VA

Recipe Consultant: Wendy Napolitano, Virginia Beach, VA

Printing: Liskey & Sons Printing, Norfolk, VA

First Edition, Volume 1   Library of Congress Catalog Card Number: 96-96208

ISBN 0-9652142-0-6

Table of Contents

Welcome to

Culinary Artists: Tidewater's Regional Chefs

This compilation of recipes from over twenty-five of Tidewater's most revered chefs allows us to venture into their kitchen tabernacles to experience selected signature recipes, savory sauces and delectable desserts.

While preparing these recipes in your own kitchen, you'll be privy to that venerable mystique these culinary artists enjoy. Like the world's most notable chefs of the past, these men and women realize their passions through the romance of cooking. Some radical, others slightly drifting but never loosing sight of their classical backgrounds, a comparison hails to celebrated ancestors performing culinary magic for European royalty, fabulous artists, great statesmen, and theatrical and musical personalities throughout centuries. Chefs' audiences have not really changed over the years, they just emerge from a different time and a new day.

The United States flourishes with regional cuisines. Maine gloats over its boiled lobsters and clam chowder, Louisiana swears by its Creole and Cajun dishes, and Texas boasts about its barbeque. But Tidewater's Chesapeake Bay with its adjacent estuaries and nearby Atlantic Ocean provides local chefs with an abundant harvest with which to create. The excitement of this bounty is richly reflected in the recipes found in this volume. The message from these chefs is clear: Whenever possible, use local products to give your creations the regional flair they so richly deserve.

During the undertaking of this project cooperation between chef and author has been extraordinary – so much so that volume two will soon make it's appearance. Use this cookbook as your guide to culinary adventure. This is an eclectic mix of magnificent recipes that will invoke a desire to fulfill any and all of your culinary wishes. *Culinary Artists: Tidewater's Regional Chefs* will enhance your knowledge of professional practices and bring that sought after taste to your home table. Where egotism and competition once stood, culinary splendor is now shared.

Bon Appétit!

Cory Beisel

501 City Grill, VA Beach

 For the past 19 years Chef Cory Beisel has been carrying on his culinary affair with Virginia Beach diners from his start cooking hamburgers at The Raven when he was 15 years old, to his current locale at 501 City Grill. "After high school I worked as a sauté cook at The Princess Anne Country Club. I worked alongside some wonderfully talented chefs and found it very exciting. That's when I seriously thought about becoming a chef."

Chef Beisel attended the Culinary Institute of America in Hyde Park, New York, returning to the Tidewater area for an apprenticeship at Kings Mill Country Club. After graduation from the institute, he came back to Virginia Beach to open his own restaurant. "In my head I had a plan I wanted to put together. I wanted my own place, and your best chance to succeed at opening your own restaurant is in your own hometown, where you know people."

From there, Chef Beisel and his partner Mike Atkinson opened several restaurants starting with South Beach Tavern. Three years later they opened Boogie's and then 501 City Grill. After experiencing grand success with 501 City Grill, they opened The Big Tomato but later sold it to concentrate all their efforts back on 501 City Grill. "I'm a chef to make a living. The Big Tomato was a success, but it was diminutive. It takes the same amount of energy to run a small restaurant as it does a large one."

Chef Beisel insists the best direction a cook can receive is through the media and through travel. "The media available to serious cooks today is a wonderful source of knowledge. Traveling is another great way to see what is out there. . . you can adapt what you learn and see, to what pleases you."

At 501 City Grill, you'll enjoy the attention given to fresh products—never frozen. An avid believer in farm-fresh quality, Chef Beisel stresses the importance of using food for what it is and not masking its primary flavor. "Sometimes people can get a little out-of-control with combinations." The menu Cory and Mike have perfected displays a variety of contemporary fusion cuisines, an extensive wine list, and a dessert selection designed to please anyone possessing a confectionery craving. "At 501 City Grill, we are here to serve and fulfill everyone's needs. I'm not going to be happy if I can't make my customers happy."

In an open kitchen, it is imperative that the showmen of the performance are costumed correctly, and to Chef Beisel that means starchy whites. Chef Beisel proudly proclaims that everyone who works at 501 City Grill exhibits 100 percent effort while on the clock. "I think the key to having a good working relationship with your employees is to never appear to be above anyone. I would never ask anyone to do anything here that I wouldn't do myself."

Cory feels his definition of eating out goes further than most, expressing that the experience should be a mini-vacation. "You should always eat whatever you want, you should be totally happy with everything, and all of your expectations should be met through the food, wine and service."

To please a following of loyal customers, Chef Beisel gives his all to cooking and menu design. Trendy, adventurous appetizers and meals are available on a specialty board, and the consistent *savoir faire* of Chef Beisel ensures customer satisfaction. "You'll always find me here because my clientele wants to see me here. I really love to cook, and I not only want to meet your expectations, I'll do my very best to surpass them!"

Black Bean and Sausage Gumbo

2 red peppers, diced

2 green peppers, diced

4 stalks celery, diced

1½ red onions, diced

1½ tablespoons chopped fresh garlic

1 teaspoon olive oil

Seasoning Mix (recipe to follow)

1 cup cooked, diced andouille sausage

¾ cup cooked black beans

2 quarts chicken stock

3 tablespoons flour mixed with ½ cup water

1½ cups canned crushed tomatoes

In a large, heavy pot sauté peppers, celery, onions and garlic in olive oil until soft. Add half of Seasoning Mix to the pot. Add sausage and black beans to the pot and mix well. Add chicken stock and mix well. Add remaining Seasoning Mix and bring to a boil.

Thicken gumbo with flour and water mixture. Add crushed tomatoes. Adjust seasonings to taste. **Serves 10**

Seasoning Mix

1 teaspoon rubbed sage	2 dashes salt
1 teaspoon marjoram	1 dash garlic powder
1 teaspoon oregano	1 dash cumin
½ teaspoon white pepper	1 dash basil
½ teaspoon thyme	
½ teaspoon cayenne pepper	
2 dashes black pepper	

Combine all ingredients and mix well.

Pan-Seared Tuna Fillet with Goat Cheese, Black Beans and Summer Salsa

Summer Salsa (recipe to follow)

2 (6 ounce) pan-seared tuna fillets

2 cups cooked black beans

6 ounces goat cheese, crumbled

2 fried blue corn tortilla shells (keep flat)

Garnish: sour cream and scallions

Prepare Summer Salsa and set aside. Pan-sear tuna fillets and keep warm.

To assemble, ladle half of the black beans onto a fried tortilla shell. Crumble half of the goat cheese on top of black beans. Layer a tuna fillet on top of cheese, and top with salsa and garnish. Repeat for second serving. **Serves 2**

Summer Salsa

1 large onion, small dice

2 medium ripe tomatoes, small dice

1 tablespoon cilantro, chopped

1½ tablespoons canned, chopped jalapeños

1 roasted green pepper, small dice

1 roasted red pepper, small dice

½ cup vegetable oil

juice of 1 lemon

juice of 1 lime

salt and pepper to taste

Combine all ingredients and mix well.

Poached Chesapeake Rockfish in Sake and Ginger with Horseradish Mashed Potatoes and Sesame Spinach

1¼ cups fish stock
¼ cup sake
1 tablespoon crushed garlic
1 tablespoon grated ginger
1 tablespoon soy sauce
4 (6 ounce) rockfish fillets
pinch of salt
pinch of white pepper

In a large sauté pan bring fish stock, sake, garlic, ginger, and soy sauce to a simmer. Season rockfish fillets with salt and white pepper. Add rockfish fillets to pan. Cook approximately 4 minutes on each side. Remove fillets and keep warm.

Reduce sauce to desired consistency. Strain and set aside.

To assemble each, place a serving of Horseradish Mashed Potatoes (recipe to follow) in the middle of a plate. Top the potatoes with the poached rockfish and then the Sesame Spinach (recipe to follow). Spoon sauce around the potatoes.
Serves 4

Horseradish Mashed Potatoes

4 potatoes, peeled and boiled until soft
pinch of salt
pinch of white pepper
prepared horseradish to taste
hot skim milk

Place potatoes, salt, white pepper and horseradish in a bowl. Mash ingredients together. Add some hot skim milk at small intervals, whipping potatoes until desired consistency is obtained. Adjust seasoning.

Sesame Spinach

1 bunch fresh spinach
½ teaspoon sesame oil
4 tablespoons sesame seeds, toasted

Wash spinach in ice water. Remove thick stems and pat dry. In a nonstick sauté pan add sesame oil and spinach, and cook until wilted. Toss with sesame seeds.

501 Virginia Crab Cakes with Curried Yogurt Peach Sauce

Crab Cakes

Curried Yogurt Peach Sauce (recipe to follow)

1¼ ounces fresh white bread
  (approximately 1½ slices)

3 egg whites

1 tablespoon low-fat mayonnaise

1½ tablespoons fresh lemon juice

1 teaspoon dry sherry

3 drops Tabasco Sauce

1½ teaspoons Worcestershire Sauce

1 teaspoon curry powder

1 teaspoon ground white pepper

1 teaspoon ground mustard

1 teaspoon paprika

½ teaspoon cayenne pepper

3 tablespoons minced fresh cilantro

1 tablespoon prepared horseradish

1½ pounds fresh lump crabmeat, picked over

2 teaspoons olive oil

Prepare Curried Yogurt Peach Sauce and chill until ready to use.

Place white bread in a food processor and process into soft pieces. Set aside.

In a medium bowl combine all ingredients except crabmeat, olive oil and bread crumbs.

Carefully add crabmeat and bread crumbs. Toss with a fork, taking care not to break up the crabmeat lumps.

Shape the crab mixture into 10 cakes and place on a baking sheet lined with wax paper.

Refrigerate for at least 20 minutes to dry out the cakes slightly. (The cakes can be made up to 1 day in advance if covered with plastic wrap and refrigerated.)

In a 10-inch nonstick skillet, heat 1 teaspoon of olive oil over medium temperature. Sauté 5 of the crab cakes until golden brown, approximately 3 minutes on each side. Remove from pan, set aside and keep warm. Add remaining teaspoon of olive oil to the pan and sauté remaining crab cakes. Serve immediately with Curried Yogurt Peach Sauce.
Makes 10 Cakes

Curried Yogurt Peach Sauce

1 cup plain nonfat yogurt

zest and juice of 3 lemons

3 tablespoons diced peaches (canned or fresh)

pinch of salt

pinch of white pepper

pinch of cayenne pepper

1 tablespoon curry powder

1 tablespoon olive oil

Place all ingredients except olive oil into a blender and purée. While blender is on, slowly add oil until completely absorbed. Keep chilled.

Warm Asparagus with Goat Cheese Au Gratin on Tomato-Basil Coulis

Tomato-Basil Coulis (recipe to follow)

12 thin asparagus spears, blanched

2 ½ ounces goat cheese, crumbled

¼ cup bread crumbs

1 cup arugula leaves

Garnish: lemon zest

Prepare and chill Tomato-Basil Coulis.

Preheat oven to 500°.

In 2 baking pans stack 6 asparagus spears in each. Top each with goat cheese and bread crumbs. Place in oven for approximately 3 minutes or until bread crumbs are brown.

To assemble, place half of the Tomato-Basil Coulis on a small plate. Top with half of arugula leaves, and one serving of the Warm Asparagus with Goat Cheese Au Gratin. Garnish with lemon zest. Repeat for second serving. **Serves 2**

Tomato-Basil Coulis

1 teaspoon olive oil

¼ teaspoon minced garlic

½ teaspoon minced onion

¼ teaspoon minced jalapeños

⅛ cup tomato paste

½ cup fresh tomato concassé

¼ cup chicken stock

½ teaspoon oregano

½ teaspoon chopped fresh cilantro

¼ cup chopped fresh basil

¼ cup red wine vinegar

In a sauté pan heat olive oil over medium-high temperature. Add garlic, onion, jalapeños and tomato paste. Stir well. Add tomato concassé and chicken stock and simmer 5 minutes. Purée mixture until smooth. Add remaining ingredients and mix well. Chill before serving. **Makes Approximately ¾ Cup**

⭐ Your Notes

5

Scott Bernheisel

Sweet Memories Catering, VA Beach

Chefs Scott Bernheisel and Jahn Sawinski

Since his early teens, Scott knew he wanted to be a chef. His first opportunity came when he knocked at the back door of a restaurant located directly behind his home in Harrisburg, Pennsylvania. "I started out washing dishes. That's when I figured out the value of hard work. From dishwashing I advanced to prep-work, bussing, buffet runner, waiter, and bartender. I did it all!"

It was both the military and Johnson & Wales University that brought Chef Scott Bernheisel to Virginia Beach. His first job after graduating culinary school was Executive Chef at the Holiday Inn in downtown Norfolk. He stayed with the Holiday Inn corporation in various Tidewater locations for more than five years. Then Chef Bernheisel began work for the Kassier family in their restaurants the Corner Market and the Bay Cafe. "I did everything at both establishments for about two years. Then, I began to realize I longed for the challenges that the large hotels presented, and I wanted to go back."

Returning to the corporate world, Chef Scott became the banquet chef at the Norfolk Waterside Marriott, and soon was promoted to Executive Chef. "In this capacity you have so much freedom to design menus, and the challenge is tailoring them for individual guests. The beauty of food is versatility. You can really show how creative you can be!"

Chef Scott met his wife Julie while working at the Norfolk Waterside Marriott. Scott gives Julie a great deal of credit for the support she extends to his business endeavors. Currently as senior catering manager at the Norfolk Waterside Marriott, she too understands the demands of the business.

From the Norfolk Waterside Marriott, Chef Scott went on to open The California Cafe, and then once again returned to the corporate world as Executive Chef at the Radisson Hotel in Virginia Beach. Finally, Scott has fulfilled his long-standing dream by opening his own catering business, Sweet Memories, in Virginia Beach, specializing in special event catering and wedding cakes.

Chef Scott finds the most rewarding part of his day is spent teaching his employees about food. "I need employees that are hungry for information. It keeps them interested and I get great satisfaction from feeling that I have enriched yet another person in the culinary field." Chef Scott wants to spread his message and bring everyone to the culinary cutting edge. "If you enrich the lives of your kitchen employees, your entire kitchen can come up a level."

Chef Scott has honorable work ethics, and he makes sure that all of his employees share in his values. He looks for everyone to show up on time and give an honest day's work for an honest day's pay. He also expects high-quality food to be presented in an artful manner. Although he maintains exacting standards, Chef Scott lives in a realistic world and emphasizes teaching his assistants to balance food basics with new technology.

Cooking is just one part of being a chef. Chefs must also use their business abilities to find ways to produce the best products while remaining profitable. "You can't be a successful chef if you don't clear a profit."

Even in his spare time, you'll find Scott using his talents to the fullest. Whether he is donating his time preparing a first-class holiday buffet for those in need or making a special wedding cake for a very special bride, Scott finds every venture he undertakes rewarding, and sometimes he expects only a smile in return.

For both the home and commercial chef, Scott cannot preach enough about starting with a clean kitchen. "Cooking can and should be fun, but you've got to do your chores first. You have to adhere to sanitation regulations or cooking can become a very dangerous practice." This goes hand-in-hand with using quality products. "If you use old strawberries to make a strawberry sauce, you are going to get an old strawberry sauce!"

Greenshell Mussel Appetizer with Thai Ginger Broth

⅛ teaspoon crushed garlic

⅛ teaspoon finely chopped shallots

1 whole leek, sliced

1 teaspoon olive oil

1 cup Thai Ginger Broth (recipe to follow)

16 greenshell mussels

8 toast points

Prepare Thai Ginger Broth and keep warm.

Sauté garlic, shallots and leek in olive oil. Add Thai Ginger Broth and mussels. Poach until warm and mussel shells open. Serve in a large, warm bowl and garnish with toast points. **Serves 2**

Thai Ginger Broth

3 tablespoons chopped garlic

½ pound fresh ginger, peeled and chopped

3 tablespoons chopped shallots

1 tablespoon olive oil

1 cup white wine

4 cups fish stock

3 tablespoons Thai seasoning

Sauté garlic, ginger and shallots in olive oil. Add white wine and allow to reduce by half. Add fish stock and Thai seasoning. Simmer for 1 hour. Strain.

Chef's Special Pasta

angel hair pasta, 4 servings

2 tablespoons butter

1 tablespoon oil

½ pound smoked salmon, large dice

12 medium shrimp, large dice

½ pound calamari, cleaned and cut into rings

1½ tablespoons chopped fresh garlic

½ pound fresh spinach, chopped

4 artichoke hearts cut into ⅛ths

½ cup sliced black olives

1 cup diced tomatoes

4 tablespoons lemon juice

1½ cups white wine

Cook pasta according to package directions. Rinse, chill, and set aside.

Heat butter and oil in a skillet. Add smoked salmon and shrimp and sauté approximately 3 minutes. Add calamari and sauté for approximately 1 minute. Add remaining ingredients. Cook and reduce sauce until thickened. Gently stir in pasta, toss and reheat thoroughly. Serve immediately. **Serves 4**

Grilled Romaine Caesar

¾ *cup red wine vinegar*

¾ *cup olive oil*

1 head Romaine lettuce

1 red pepper, roasted (method to follow)

1 cup olive oil, as needed

12 peeled cloves of garlic, roasted (method to follow)

1 cup croutons

¾ *cup shredded Parmesan cheese*

4 anchovy fillets

1 cup Creamy Pepper Caesar dressing

Garnish: fresh cracked black pepper

    Heat grill.

    In a shallow pan, whip vinegar and olive oil together. Set aside.

    Tear off undesirable large, wilted leaves from head of Romaine lettuce and discard. Keeping head of lettuce whole, wash thoroughly.

    With a sharp knife, carefully cut head of lettuce in half lengthwise, cutting right through the heart to keep the leaves together. Dredge the center of the lettuce in the oil and vinegar mixture and place on a hot grill for about 15-30 seconds. (**Caution:** *When oil hits the flame, it will rise up over the lettuce.*) The lettuce should have grill marks on it, but should still be crisp.

    Place on a plate and chill for 30 minutes. Carefully remove grate from the grill.

    Rub the red pepper with olive oil. Using long-handled tongs, place pepper on hot coals and char on all sides. Remove pepper from coals and place in a brown paper bag and close. Let rest for 30 minutes. Remove from bag and peel blackened skin off, cut in half, remove seeds, and julienne.

    Preheat oven to 250°. To roast garlic, place peeled garlic cloves in a small container or pan. Pour just enough olive oil over cloves to cover them, and bake for 1 hour. Cloves should be soft and golden brown when finished. Remove from oil and chill for 30 minutes.

    To assemble salad, place grilled head of Romaine on plate with grilled side up. Top with roasted garlic, roasted red pepper strips, shredded Parmesan cheese, and croutons. Drizzle Caesar dressing on salad, place a criss-cross of anchovy fillets on top. Garnish with fresh cracked black pepper around rim of plate. **Serves 2**

Delmonico Schmearkasse

2 (14 ounce) Delmonico steaks, thick cut

1 cup Worcestershire Sauce

½ *cup chili powder*

1 teaspoon salt

1 teaspoon pepper

½ *cup red wine*

½ *cup olive oil*

2 teaspoons onion powder

¼ *cup red wine vinegar*

2 teaspoons cumin

3 cloves garlic, crushed

    Set steaks aside.

    Combine all other ingredients in a bowl and whisk together. Allow marinade to sit for 30 minutes and whisk again. Rub the marinade into steaks and refrigerate a minimum of 1 hour. (*Steaks are best if allowed to marinate overnight.*) Bake steaks on a sheet pan in a 350° oven, or grill, until desired degree of doneness is achieved. **Serves 2**

Pecan-Encrusted Red Snapper with Grapefruit Salsa

Grapefruit Salsa (recipe to follow)
1 cup grapefruit juice
1 tablespoon cornstarch mixed with a little water
1 tablespoon butter
2 (6-8 ounce) red snapper fillets
½ cup all purpose flour
2 eggs, whipped
½ cup chopped pecans

One day ahead, prepare Grapefruit Salsa.

In a small saucepan, add grapefruit juice and the cornstarch mixture. Bring to a boil. Keep this grapefruit sauce warm.

Preheat oven to 400°. In a sauté pan, heat butter. Dredge fillets (meat side only) in flour, then in whipped eggs and then pecans. Sauté meat side of fillet for 1 minute. Pecans should begin to brown. Finish cooking snapper in oven for approximately 8-10 minutes. Fish should be done but not overcooked.

To assemble, strain grapefruit salsa and place half of salsa on a serving plate. Place cooked red snapper on top of salsa with skin side up and finish with a spoonful of warm grapefruit sauce. Repeat for second serving. **Serves 2**

Grapefruit Salsa

1 green pepper, small dice
1 red pepper, small dice
1 medium red onion, diced
¼ cucumber, peeled, seeded, small dice
2 cups grapefruit juice
5 tablespoons sugar
1 pink grapefruit peeled, sections removed, seeded, membrane removed, chopped

In a bowl combine diced peppers, onion, cucumber, grapefruit juice and sugar. Let set overnight and then add grapefruit sections. Strain before serving.

Creamed Oysters

1 tablespoon butter
1 large leek, julienne
2 large shallots, chopped
½ ounce morel mushrooms, cut in half
10 select oysters, shucked
¾ cup heavy cream
1 ounce frozen chopped spinach
salt and pepper to taste
Garnish: grilled crusty bread slices

Melt butter in sauté pan over high temperature. Add leeks, shallots and mushrooms. Sauté 1 minute. Add oysters, heavy cream and spinach. Bring to boil and reduce for 3 minutes. Add salt and pepper to taste.

Serve 5 oysters and half of cream sauce in each bowl along with grilled crusty bread slices. **Serves 2**

Stingray Point Fillet

2 (8 ounce) beef fillets trimmed of all fat

salt and pepper to taste

8 oysters, raw

flour for dredging

egg wash

bread crumbs for dredging

oil for frying

¼ cup mushrooms, chopped

1 whole leek, chopped

2 tablespoons butter

1 cup heavy cream

Grill fillet with salt and pepper to taste. Heat oil until very hot. Dredge raw oysters in flour, then egg wash, then in bread crumbs and then fry in hot oil until done.

To make sauce, sauté mushrooms and leek in butter with salt and pepper to taste. Add heavy cream and reduce until thick.

To serve, spoon sauce on plate, place fillet on sauce and garnish with fried oysters.

Optional garnish: Slice onions very thin, fluff in flour lightly seasoned with paprika, salt and pepper then drop in hot oil and cook until crispy. Serve on top of oysters. **Serves 2**

David Blackstock

Crackers, Norfolk

An inherited sign in the window determined the name for David Blackstock's stylish establishment located on 21st street in Ghent. Born in Kingston, England, Chef Blackstock received the bulk of his training in Europe working for such grandly established companies as the Claridges Hotel, and the Connaught Hotel within the acclaimed Savoy Group.

One of the lucky few to meet royalty, David was privileged to cater a banquet for Prince Charles and Earl Mountbatten at the Royal Thames Yacht Club. He also hosted a buffet for the infamous billiards players Fred and Joe Davis, and catered "Breakfast on the Radio," an on-air talk show that featured distinguished guests such as Omar Sharrif. Being in the right place at the right time has served David well. While working a room service shift at the Claridges Hotel, he caught Frank Sinatra practicing a few golf shots in the hallway!

Along his career path, David has developed a knack for refurbishing restaurant kitchens, turning consternation into culinary composure and success. While working at one of his restaurants in England, David met his wife-to-be, Ann. It was love at first sight. "She was on vacation in England with one of her friends. We soon married and I followed her back to Norfolk."

As it is for most chefs, dear old mom was David's cooking inspiration. "Whatever she cooked, it always tasted good. I have always been fascinated with food and wine. I have been drawn to it ever since I was a child." Enthralled with the sight, smell and sound of foods being transformed from their raw state into the finished product, David compares the kitchen process to musical orchestration – it is soulful and self-feeding.

Chef Blackstock feels that honesty is the best policy: it's always tempting to buy a cheaper substitution, but if you are honest about your abilities and discriminating with your products, you should experience great success in the kitchen. "I always try to practice the culinary art as often as I can, and to the best of my ability. Most important, I am a believer in passing on my skills and achieved merits to others."

With limited seating, reservations at Crackers are always essential. David says he enjoys working in a restaurant this size because it enables him to remain a hands-on chef and personally embellish each plate ordered. "I love this restaurant, and I think people sense that when they see me here every night working for them." A glimpse into the kitchen can be had on the way in and out of the dining room, which allows David to personally greet his customers on their way in, and thank them on their way out.

A seasoned wait-staff of two, Nadia and Mark, will expertly guide you through the menu, anticipating your needs and desires while trying to make your evening an exceptionally gratifying affair.

Crackers' small size also allows Chef Blackstock to procure the bulk of his raw materials at the grocery store, where he can carefully select his products and plan his menu according to what's fresh. "I like to do all the shopping for the restaurant myself. Purveyors are good for staple items and dry goods, but grocery stores move their merchandise quicker, so their products are fresher. I also get inspiration for new menu ideas while perusing up and down the aisles."

The most oft-requested food on Chef Blackstock's menu is fish. "Fresh fish is so easy to get in this area, and I like to take advantage of that." David also prides himself on the free-range products he serves and his personally selected wine list. "Food, health and happiness are united entities. There's nothing more soul-destroying than having to eat something you don't like." At Crackers, you can practice "cuisine spontaneity" and order anything on the menu cooked your way – or ask for it David's favorite way!

13

Grilled Lamb

Red Wine Marinade (recipe to follow)
4 (6-8 ounce) lamb steaks, bone in or out
vegetable oil
1½ cups good red wine (Pinot Noir)
2 sprigs rosemary
¼ cup honey
1 cup au jus or demi-glace

Marinade lamb steaks for 4 hours in Red Wine Marinade.

Heat grill. Oil meat and grill over hot grill 7-8 minutes per side until medium or medium-rare. Let rest 10-15 minutes in a warm place.

Combine wine and rosemary in a saucepan and reduce wine by ⅔. Add honey and bring to a boil. Add demi-glace or au jus and reduce again until sauce reaches a smooth coating consistency and has a rich ruby color. Discard rosemary. Serve sauce over lamb. **Serves 4**

Red Wine Marinade

1 cup red wine
½ cup olive oil
1 clove garlic, minced
1 sprig rosemary
1 bay leaf

Mix all ingredients together thoroughly.

Crème Brûlée

2 cups vanilla flavored sugar*
1 cup half & half
1 cup heavy whipping cream
pinch of saffron threads
5 jumbo egg yolks
Garnish: kiwi or raspberries

Place sugar, creams and saffron into a medium-size, stainless-steel saucepan. Whisk gently over low temperature to combine ingredients. Raise heat and bring to a boil.

Meanwhile, whisk egg yolks in a bowl. Add a cup or so of the hot cream mixture. Whisk quickly to incorporate. Transfer incorporated mixture back into saucepan with remaining mixture, whisking continuously until slight "trails" form in the custard. When this state is achieved, pour custard into four bowls or gelatin dishes. Refrigerate until set.

To glaze top of Crème Brûlée, scatter an even layer of sugar over surface of custard and apply torch flame evenly until desired caramelization is achieved. Don't forget that the sugar will continue to cook a little bit after the heat is taken away. If you don't have a torch, melt some sugar in a heavy pan until golden, then carefully pour over custards.

Garnish with fruit such as kiwi or raspberries. **Serves 4**

*Chef's Note: To make vanilla sugar, place a few vanilla beans with sugar in a closed jar and let sit for a few weeks.

Cajun Pasta

1 (6 ounce) boneless chicken breast, diced

½ onion, sliced

1 link andouille sausage, sliced thin

3 teaspoons Cajun Spice Mix (recipe to follow)

3 tablespoons crushed tomatoes

3 tablespoons au jus

2 tablespoon heavy cream

8 medium shrimp, peeled

½ bell pepper, julienne

1 scallion, sliced thin

salt and black pepper to taste

½ pound cooked pasta (penne, shells or fusilli)

Grill or sauté chicken breast until almost done.

Meanwhile, over medium-high temperature, sauté onions and sausage together until nicely browned. Add chicken breast. Add Cajun Spice Mix and stir well. Add crushed tomatoes, au jus, and cream. Bring to a boil. Add shrimp and cook for approximately 2-3 minutes or until shrimp is done. Add bell pepper and scallion. Season with salt and pepper.

Toss with your choice of cooked pasta and serve. **Serves 2**

Chef's Note: This dish can be made spicy or mild. Use more Cajun Spice Mix to make this recipe hotter.

Cajun Spice Mix

2 tablespoons paprika	*1 teaspoon black pepper*
1 tablespoon cumin	*½ teaspoon salt*
1 teaspoon thyme	*2 teaspoons cayenne pepper*

Combine all ingredients and mix well.

Tuna with Cilantro Sauce

4 (6 ounce) tuna steaks

olive oil

Cilantro Sauce (recipe to follow)

Lightly oil tuna steaks. Grill or pan-sear until medium-rare or desired degree of doneness is achieved. Keep warm.
Prepare Cilantro Sauce
Pour Cilantro Sauce over tuna steaks. Serve immediately.
Serves 4

Cilantro Sauce

2 cloves garlic, minced

small piece of ginger, minced

½ cup soy sauce

¼ cup sherry

4 ounces butter, cut into small pieces

⅛ cup chopped cilantro

dash of lime juice

In a non-reactive pan mix garlic, ginger, soy sauce and sherry. Bring to a boil, reduce temperature slightly and whisk in butter one piece at a time. Add cilantro and lime juice.

Chicken Madras

2 tablespoons vegetable oil

2 tablespoons melted butter

4 (6 ounce) chicken breasts

Curry Spice Mix (recipe to follow)

2 cloves garlic, minced

small piece of bay leaf

1 cup heavy cream

¼ cup diced tomato

¼ cup diced red onion

1 tablespoon curry powder

Basmati rice or couscous, 4 servings

Garnish: mango chutney, lime pickle

  and minted yogurt

Preheat oven to 375-400°. Prepare Curry Spice Mix and set aside.

Mix together oil and melted butter. Add oil/butter mixture to an oven-proof pan and lightly sauté chicken over medium temperature 3 minutes. (Keep the chicken from browning. You want it to remain colorless.)

Coat chicken evenly with Curry Spice Mix and return to the pan. Add garlic and bay leaf to the pan. Bake for 20-25 minutes until the juices are snow white. Remove chicken from pan.

Deglaze pan on top of stove with cream and reduce until thickened. Add tomato, onion and curry powder.

Serve over boiled Basmati rice or couscous and accompany with mango chutney, lime pickle and minted yogurt. **Serves 4**

Curry Spice Mix

(in heaping teaspoons)

3 paprika

3 tumeric

2 cilantro

1 garam masala

1 cayenne pepper

Mix all ingredients together thoroughly.

Amy Brandt

The Lucky Star, VA Beach

In 1985 Chef Amy Brandt followed her heart from New York to Virginia and, luckily for Tidewater residents, she decided to stay. Her first cooking experiences were in nondescript restaurants in the area, but her creative interests were piqued and cooking became a career when she had the opportunity to work with Meredith Nicolls. With a natural talent for art, her canvas soon became the plate, and she opened The Lucky Star in 1989.

Chef Brandt graduated from Johnson & Wales University in Rhode Island and quickly received recognition as a culinary artist.

"It happened before I knew it. Being a chef is very hard work, and I think that anyone who wants to get into this business needs to know that."

Amy graciously acknowledges the strong showing of regional culinary talent and admires chefs that use and promote local products. That's easy to do with Tidewater's long growing season and the wealth of the Atlantic Ocean and Chesapeake Bay. "I also like straightforward chefs that aren't fussy and just cook good food – real food."

The Lucky Star has a small staff, and Chef Brandt insists that everyone who works at the restaurant be career-oriented and dedicated to the job. As a working chef she is on-site every day, handling everything from the front to the back of the house. While aiming not to be too exclusive, The Lucky Star does coddle to food knowledgeable customers. "Some foods on the menu are very audacious. However there are a few less adventurous menu items to satisfy the prudent diner." Chef Brandt cooks a variety of foods, changing the menu seasonally and showcasing local items whenever possible. "Whatever I'm cooking, I strive for it to be good, creative food using only quality products."

Chef Brandt appreciates the importance of a good, sound diet and lifestyle, and endeavors to adhere to a vegetarian regime. Even as a full-time chef, Amy finds time to enjoy a few hobbies including just about anything that can be done outdoors. "Keeping physically fit is very important to me, and I make an effort to do it."

Her kitchen principle is simple – keep it clean and organized. The home cook can be just as appreciated as the commercial chef. Although the home cook's audience is usually the same every night, he or she can create chef-quality sensations by following professional practices. "Obviously, you have to prepare ahead of time. If you can master that practice, you've got the game won."

Knowing the recipe is extremely important. "If you are going down your list of ingredients and methods while you are in the cooking process and find you are missing something or don't know how to complete a step, you can end up with a real mess on your hands." Hoping to spark creativity, Chef Brandt insists that cooks should never be afraid to substitute ingredients – within reason. The recipe should only be used as a guideline for catering to your family or your guest's tastes, "but always remain realistic and cook within your limitations for the best results."

Mussels Steamed with Leeks, Potatoes, Cream and Fresh Herbs

2 cups dry white wine

4 bay leaves

½ teaspoon chopped fresh rosemary

½ teaspoon chopped fresh thyme

dash of cayenne pepper

2-3 pounds mussels

3 tablespoons clarified butter

4 large cloves of garlic, sliced thin

1 leek, trimmed of dark green leaves, sliced thin

4 tablespoons flour

1 cup chicken stock

2 tablespoons cognac

3 cups peeled, diced potatoes

1 cup seeded, diced tomatoes

1 cup heavy cream

⅓ cup rough chopped parsley

½ teaspoon freshly ground black pepper

French bread

Combine first 6 ingredients in a large pot with a tight-fitting lid. Bring to a boil and steam over high temperature until the mussel shells open. Remove from heat and transfer the mussels, reserving cooking liquid to a large bowl. Cover and keep warm.

Heat the clarified butter in a large saucepan. Add garlic and leek and sauté briefly. Add the flour and stir in completely. Add the reserved cooking liquid, chicken stock, cognac, potatoes and tomatoes. Boil about 6 minutes. Add the cream, parsley and black pepper. Simmer about 2 minutes and pour over mussels.

Serve immediately with crusty French bread. **Serves 4**

Autumn Bisque

¼ cup canola oil

2 yellow onions, julienne

2 butternut squash, peeled, seeded, large dice

4 carrots, peeled and chopped

2 apples, cored, medium dice

8 cups chicken stock

2 russet potatoes, peeled, medium dice

1 teaspoon dried herbes de Provençe

½ teaspoon white pepper

1 cup heavy cream

salt and white pepper to taste

2 tablespoons Calvados or Applejack spirits

1 cup sour cream

Garnish: 1 apple, small dice and 1 pear, fine dice

Over medium temperature, heat a large stock pot. Add the oil and onions. Sauté onions until they begin to caramelize.

Add the squash, carrots, apples, stock and potatoes. Bring to a boil and then reduce to a simmer. Cook until the vegetables are soft.

Purée the bisque using a processor and return to the burner. Re-heat at medium temperature. Add the herbs de Provençe, white pepper and heavy cream. Season to taste with salt and white pepper.

In a separate bowl, combine Calvados and sour cream. To serve, ladle hot soup into pre-warmed bowls. Spoon the sour cream mixture onto the soup and garnish with diced apples and pears. **Serves 8**

Butch's Deviled Crab

1½ cups celery, fine chop

1½ cups yellow onion, fine chop

2 ounces butter

1 cup bread crumbs

1½ tablespoons Old Bay Seasoning

1½ tablespoons Tabasco Sauce

2 tablespoons Worcestershire Sauce

2 tablespoons sherry

1 cup heavy cream

½ pound backfin crabmeat, picked over

1 pound claw crabmeat, picked over

8 cleaned crab shells

Garnish: Spanish paprika

Preheat oven to 400°.

In a large skillet, sauté celery and onion in butter until onion is translucent.

In a large bowl, mix bread crumbs and Old Bay Seasoning together. Add Tabasco, Worcestershire, sherry, heavy cream, and cooked celery and onions. Blend well. Add the picked over crabmeat and stir gently.

Portion into 8 servings and fill cleaned crab shells with the mixture. Bake until brown, approximately 10 minutes. Garnish with Spanish paprika. **Serves 8**

Santa Fe Brownies

6 ounces butter

1 cup packed brown sugar

¾ pound bittersweet chocolate, broken into
    small pieces

1 tablespoon unsweetened cocoa powder

3 eggs

2 tablespoons instant coffee

2 tablespoons dark rum

1 teaspoon ground cinnamon

1 tablespoon chili powder

1 cup flour

pinch of salt

¾ cup pine nuts

Preheat oven to 350°. Butter and flour a 9x9-inch baking pan.

In a saucepan combine the butter and brown sugar. Heat over medium temperature, cooking until the brown sugar has dissolved. Remove from heat.

Place chocolate pieces and cocoa in a mixing bowl. Add the butter/sugar mixture. Using a mixer, mix on a low speed until the chocolate is melted.

In a separate bowl, combine the eggs, instant coffee, rum, cinnamon and chili powder. From this mixture, add what would be the equivalent of one egg at a time to the chocolate mixture, mixing and scraping down the bowl after each addition. Add the flour and salt and mix again. Add the pine nuts, and pour batter into prepared pan. Bake for 25-30 minutes or until a toothpick inserted in the center comes out clean. **Serves 6**

Chicken Braised with Prunes and Vinegar

½ pound bacon, cut into ¼" pieces

oil for sautéing, if needed

2 (2 pound) chickens, cut into pieces

2 cups flour, seasoned

10 cloves garlic, sliced thin

1 yellow onion, julienne

4 stalks celery, diced

2 carrots, diced

2 cups chicken stock

4 bay leaves

3 cups red wine

½ cup red wine vinegar

½ cup balsamic vinegar

½ teaspoon dried thyme

½ teaspoon dried sage

½ teaspoon dried marjoram

2 cups pitted prunes, chopped

cooked rice, 4 servings

    Preheat oven to 375°.

    In a large Dutch oven with a tight-fitting lid, cook the bacon over medium temperature until crisp. Remove and set aside. Increase the temperature to medium-high. Add oil if the pan appears dry. Dredge chicken pieces in the seasoned flour and place in the pan. Cook chicken until browned on all sides. Remove chicken and set aside.

    In the same pan, briefly sauté the garlic until slightly browned. Add the onion, celery and carrots and sauté briefly. Add the remaining ingredients and bring to a simmer.

    Return chicken pieces to the pan and cover tightly. Place in oven and bake for 1 hour. Serve with rice. **Serves 4**

Smoked Fish Spread for Bruschetta

1¼ pounds smoked fish, preferably tuna

1½ teaspoons fresh rosemary, chopped very fine

1 red bell pepper, roasted, peeled and diced

1 tablespoon red wine vinegar

½ bunch parsley, rough chop

pinch of crushed red pepper flakes

½ cup mayonnaise

¼ cup sour cream

salt and fresh ground black pepper to taste

bruschetta

    Crumble the smoked fish into a large mixing bowl. Add the remaining ingredients and mix well. Adjust the seasoning with salt and freshly ground black pepper. Serve with bruschetta. **Serves 12**

Timothy Brown and Deanna Freridge

Toques Creative Catering, VA Beach

Two fellow New Yorkers have proven they've got what it takes to be "hats above the crowd" at Toques Creative Catering in Virginia Beach. Chef co-owners Deanna Freridge and Timothy Brown can turn any gathering into a grandiose occasion with their magical formula for entertainment success. At Toques Creative Catering the emphasis is definitely on creativity. Specializing in gourmet hors d'oeuvres and glorious desserts, the talents of these two chefs are magnificently displayed in their works of comestible art. Toques Creative Catering will design a unique menu for any occasion, top-dollar or conservative.

Chef Timothy Brown has lived in the Tidewater area for 11 years and has worked with local greats Frank Farillo and Monroe Duncan. A Johnson & Wales, Norfolk, graduate, he has returned to the university to instruct students in various aspects of the culinary field. "To be a great chef, you must understand ingredients, where they come from, how they are used, their flavors and what they are compatible with." Chef Brown adds that a successful chef also has to understand portion and cost analy-

sis to survive. "Most important, if people realize that cooking is simply a combination of different methods, they'll easily grasp culinary procedures and will be able to make or create anything."

Chef Deanna Freridge was born in Queens, New York, and currently resides in Virginia Beach. Understanding the needs of her dining public requires an extensive knowledge of how people like to entertain. Her rewards are earned by making her customers happy, and that means pleasing a lot of people. "If I take pride in my work, I know it will speak for itself. The crowds we aim to please are people who love to eat exciting and interesting food, and that makes my job fascinating." Chef Freridge's mentors in the culinary business are chefs who are education-oriented, entertaining, experimental and utilize time-honored practices.

As a chef, Deanna knows what it takes to turn any product into a successful dining delight, and she offers home cooks a few easy hints: "Keep focused, don't be afraid to try new things, and learn from your mistakes."

Chef Freridge finds the culinary field to be extremely rewarding and hopes that aspiring chefs find food service to be an exciting and fulfilling career choice. "There are so many different avenues one can take within this industry. All you have to do is explore them!"

Both chefs agree that using the freshest ingredients is of utmost importance. As with all dining experiences, it is important to be open-minded, to savor every bite, and to really enjoy the food's presentation and tastes. While the catering business is a rewarding field, there are many factors to contend with. Caterers not only have to please their customers, but their customers' guests as well. The chefs at Toques Creative Catering strive for consistency in everything they do. "Going that extra mile for the customers keeps them coming back!"

Photographs by Stacey Haines

Bourboned Chicken Liver and Italian Sausage Pâté

1 pound chicken livers

milk for soaking chicken livers

1 pound hot or mild Italian sausage links

2 tablespoons finely chopped garlic

1 cup Kentucky bourbon

4 ounces chilled unsalted butter, cut into pats

cocktail breads

Place chicken livers in a colander and rinse with cold water. Drain well. Place livers in a bowl and add enough milk to cover them completely. Refrigerate from 2-24 hours. (This helps reduce the heavy iron flavor.)

Remove sausage from casing and place in skillet over medium temperature and cook until all pink is gone. Drain fat from skillet and place sausage in food processor. Pulse on medium until coarse. Do not over chop sausage. Place sausage in a bowl and set aside.

Strain livers from milk. Set skillet over medium temperature. Add livers and garlic and sauté until pink is almost gone. Add bourbon to the skillet to deglaze. (**CAUTION:** *Remove skillet from stove before adding bourbon*). Reduce by ¾.

Place livers in food processor. Add a few pats of butter at a time and blend on high until smooth, stopping occasionally to scrape down sides. This can be done in batches if you have a small food processor.

Fold liver mixture into cooked Italian sausage. Adjust seasoning with salt and pepper. If you like a stronger bourbon flavor, add a dash more to taste. Keep refrigerated until ready to use. Serve at room temperature with rye and pumpernickel cocktail breads. **Serves 8**

Warm Artichoke-Crab Cheese Dip

1 pound softened cream cheese

1 cup mayonnaise

½ cup grated Parmesan cheese

½ cup finely grated Gruyere or Swiss cheese

1-2 tablespoons Worcestershire Sauce

1 tablespoon lemon juice

1 teaspoon garlic powder

dash of Tabasco Sauce

1 (13 ounce) can artichoke hearts, drained, coarsely chopped

1 bunch green onions, chopped fine

1 pound lump crabmeat, picked over

crackers and garlic croustades

Preheat oven to 350°.

In a mixing bowl whip cream cheese until smooth. Add mayonnaise and blend. Add cheeses, Worcestershire, lemon juice, garlic and Tabasco. Blend until all ingredients are incorporated.

Fold in artichokes, green onions and crabmeat. Place all ingredients in ovenproof casserole dish. Bake in oven until bubbly and golden brown. Serve with crackers and garlic croustades. **Serves 8**

Sesame-Coated Pork Tenderloin with Marinated Cucumbers and Peanut Sauce

Pork Tenderloin

Marinated Cucumbers (recipe to follow)

2 tablespoons finely chopped garlic

1/2 cup black or white sesame seeds

2 tablespoons vegetable oil

2 tablespoons sesame oil

salt and pepper to taste

2 pound pork tenderloin, trimmed of fat

Peanut Sauce (recipe to follow)

Prepare Marinated Cucumbers. Chill until ready to serve. Preheat oven to 375°.

In a bowl mix together the garlic, sesame seeds, oils, salt and pepper, and coat all sides of the pork tenderloin. Bake in oven until medium or desired degree of doneness is achieved.

While tenderloin is baking, prepare Peanut Sauce.

When tenderloin is done, let it rest for a few minutes, then slice and serve with marinated cucumbers and peanut sauce. **Serves 4**

Marinated Cucumbers

1/2 cup water

1/2 cup white vinegar

1/2 cup sugar

2 tablespoons finely chopped fresh dill

3 large cucumbers

salt

3 green onions, diced

3 small green chilies, seeded, diced

To make marinade, combine water, vinegar, sugar and dill. Whisk until sugar dissolves. Set aside.

Peel cucumbers and cut in half lengthwise. With a spoon remove seeds from center. Slice crosswise into 1/2-inch slices. Set slices in colander and toss with salt. Set colander inside a bowl and refrigerate for 2 hours.

Remove cucumbers from refrigerator. Discard any liquid and place cucumbers in bowl. Pour the marinade over the cucumbers. Add onions and chilies. Refrigerate 2 hours. Serve chilled. **Serves 4**

Peanut Sauce

1 cup peanut butter

1/4 cup vegetable oil

2 tablespoons white vinegar

2 chile peppers, ground

2-3 tablespoons soy sauce

Place peanut butter in small mixing bowl and beat on medium until smooth. With beaters rotating, alternate adding remaining ingredients beginning and ending with vegetable oil. Serve at room temperature.

Peach and Pistachio Praline Tart

Pistachio Praline Crust

2¹/₂ cups pistachios, chopped fine

¹/₂ cup sugar

4 ounces melted butter

Preheat oven to 350°. Mix melted butter with pistachios and sugar and form to make a crust in a 9-inch tart pan with removable bottom. Bake in oven until light brown. Remove from oven and set aside. (May be made one day in advance.)

Peach Bavarian Cream

2 tablespoons unflavored gelatin granules

¹/₂ cup peach schnapps

¹/₂ cup whole milk

¹/₂ cup cornstarch

5 eggs

1 cup whole milk

2 ounces butter

¹/₂ cup sugar

¹/₂ cup puréed peaches

1 cup heavy whipping cream

In a double boiler off of the stove, dissolve gelatin in peach schnapps. Set aside.

In a separate bowl, mix ¹/₂ cup of cold milk with the cornstarch. Add eggs and mix. Set aside.

In a saucepan, add 1 cup of milk, the butter and the sugar and bring to a boil. Add cornstarch mixture to the butter mixture. Cook over low temperature until thick. Remove from heat.

Heat gelatin mixture until clear and add to the saucepan. Add peach purée. Place over an ice bath and cool until almost set.

Whip heavy cream. Carefully fold whipped cream into saucepan.

Pour into praline crust. Refrigerate until set.

Topping

7-8 fresh peaches, sliced paper thin

apricot or clear glaze (may be commercially purchased)

After tart is set, arrange sliced peaches on top. Melt glaze and brush top of tart. Let cool. Cut and serve. **Serves 8**

Chocolate and Peanut Butter Swirl Cheesecake

Peanut Butter Cookie Crust

4 ounces butter

$^3/_4$ cup peanut butter

$^1/_2$ cup sugar

$^1/_2$ cup brown sugar

1 egg

$1^1/_4$ cups flour

1 tablespoon baking soda

$^1/_4$ teaspoon baking powder

pinch of salt

melted butter

Preheat oven to 350°.

Mix butter and peanut butter together. Add sugars and mix well. Add egg and mix well.

In a separate bowl combine flour, baking soda, baking powder and salt. Add to mixture and stir until completely incorporated. Place approximately 2 tablespoons of dough, 3 inches apart on an ungreased cookie sheet and bake until light brown. After cookies have baked and cooled, pulverize with a little melted butter to make cookie crust crumbs.

Line a 9-inch springform pan with the cookie crumbs, forming the crust. Refrigerate for approximately 5 minutes to set.

Prepare Chocolate Cheesecake Mixture (recipe to follow) and pour onto Peanut Butter Cookie crust. Prepare Peanut Butter Cheesecake Mixture (recipe to follow) and swirl into Chocolate Cheesecake. Bake for 1 hour in a water bath.

Serves 8

Chocolate Cheesecake

$^1/_2$ cup hot coffee

1 pound semisweet chocolate, broken into pieces

$1^1/_2$ pounds cream cheese

$1^1/_2$ cups sugar

1 teaspoon salt

6 eggs

2 teaspoons vanilla

Pour hot coffee over chocolate and stir until melted.

Whip cream cheese, sugar and salt with a mixer. Slowly add eggs and vanilla. Fold in chocolate mixture. Set aside.

Peanut Butter Cheesecake

$^1/_2$ pound cream cheese

1 tablespoon unsalted butter

$^3/_4$ cup sugar

$^1/_4$ teaspoon salt

1 tablespoon flour

2 eggs

$^1/_2$ teaspoon vanilla

$^1/_2$ cup smooth peanut butter

Whip cream cheese, butter, sugar and salt with a mixer. Add flour. Slowly add eggs and vanilla. Add peanut butter and mix just until incorporated. Set aside.

Chocolate Coconut Decadence

Coconut Crust

4 ounces butter, melted

2^1/$_2$ cups shredded coconut

^{1}/$_2$ teaspoon vanilla

^{1}/$_4$ teaspoon salt

Preheat oven to 350°.

In a saucepan, melt butter over low temperature.

In a separate bowl, mix together coconut, vanilla and salt. Add melted butter and form mixture into the bottom of a 9-inch springform pan.

Bake for approximately 15 minutes or until the edges of the crust turn light brown. Let cool completely. Set aside.

Chocolate Decadence

1 pound semisweet chocolate, broken into pieces

5 ounces unsalted butter

3 eggs

1 tablespoon flour

1 tablespoon granulated sugar

In the top of a double boiler, melt chocolate and butter. Remove from heat.

In a mixing bowl, whip eggs on high speed until light and fluffy. Fold in flour and sugar.

When chocolate mixture has cooled slightly, fold into egg mixture. Pour on top of coconut crust and refrigerate for 2 hours or overnight. Remove from springform pan.

Chocolate Ganache

^{1}/$_2$ pound semisweet chocolate, chopped

2 ounces unsalted butter

2 tablespoons light corn syrup

1 cup heavy whipping cream

In a mixing bowl, combine chocolate, butter, and corn syrup. In a saucepan over medium temperature, bring cream to a boil. Pour boiling cream over chocolate mixture and stir until smooth. Set aside and let cool slightly.

Place a cooling rack over a sheet pan and place the Chocolate Decadence on the cooling rack (the sheet pan will catch the ganache drippings). Coating evenly, pour Chocolate Ganache over the Chocolate Decadence, allowing the Ganache to drip off. Reserve left over Ganache and drippings in a small bowl. Refrigerate dessert for approximately 2 hours.

White Chocolate Coconut Cookie Garnish

^{1}/$_4$ cup granulated sugar

3 tablespoons all-purpose flour

^{1}/$_4$ cup shredded coconut

2 tablespoons unsalted butter

1 ounce white chocolate

1 egg

Garnish: 1 cup toasted coconut

Preheat oven to 350°.

Mix dry ingredients together, including the coconut. In the top of a double boiler, melt butter and white chocolate. Add to the dry ingredients. Add egg and mix until incorporated. Place approximately 1 teaspoon of cookie dough onto a cookie sheet coated with a cooking spray. Spread out in a circle until it is about 3 inches in diameter.

Bake cookies until the edges are light brown. Cool slightly and carefully scrape off sheet pan. Roll cookie jelly-roll fashion and cool completely.

Dip rolled cookie half-way in ganache drippings. Let cool and garnish the edges of the cookie with toasted coconut. Place on the Chocolate Coconut Decadence at a 45° angle. **Serves 8**

Pan-Fried Chèvre Cheese Zaden

4 ounces chèvre cheese, divided into 2 portions

flour for dredging

egg wash

bread crumbs for dredging

½ cup olive oil

2 shallots, chopped

2 tablespoons pink peppercorns

1 cup heavy cream

pinch of parsley, chopped

garlic croustades

Preheat oven to 325°.

Set up breading procedure (flour, egg wash, and bread crumbs all in separate bowls). Dredge the two portions of chèvre cheese in the flour, then the egg wash and then the bread crumbs. Set aside.

Heat olive oil in a pan over medium temperature and sauté chèvre cheese until completely brown on both sides. Remove and place in oven while preparing sauce.

Remove oil from pan. Add shallots, peppercorns and heavy cream. Reduce until thickened and toss in parsley.

To serve, place sauce on plate and chèvre cheese on top. Serve with garlic croustades. **Serves 4**

Toque Exotique

$^1\!/_2$ **pound semisweet chocolate coating pieces**

$^1\!/_4$ **pound white chocolate coating pieces**

$1^1\!/_2$ **pounds White Chocolate Mousse**

   (recipe to follow)

$1^1\!/_2$ **cups raspberry sauce (recipe to follow)***

$1^1\!/_2$ **cups blackberry sauce***

$1^1\!/_2$ **cups peach sauce***

Garnish: fresh berries, mint and chocolate shards

    To assemble dessert, melt chocolate coating pieces separately over a double boiler over low temperature.

    Paint the inside of paper cupcake wrappers and refrigerate to harden. After hardened, gently peel away wrappers and you will have chocolate cups to hold the white chocolate mousse.

    To assemble each, place a small amount of all three fruit sauces on a plate.   Place filled chocolate cup on plate. Garnish with fresh berries, mint and chocolate shards or designs. **Serves 6**

Chef's Note: You can paint wrappers with all semisweet or all white chocolate, and paint on stripes with the contrasting color. You can also paint wax paper with melted chocolate coatings and break into shards or cut into designs for garnish. Use your imagination with piping, swirling, etc.

White Chocolate Mousse

$^3\!/_4$ **pound white chocolate**

2 ounces butter

2 egg yolks

2 eggs

$^1\!/_2$ **cup heavy whipping cream**

2 tablespoons granulated sugar

    Melt white chocolate and butter over a double boiler over very low temperature. Meanwhile, whip egg yolks and eggs with mixer until triple in volume, light and fluffy.

    When chocolate is melted, fold it into egg mixture and set aside.

    Whip heavy cream and sugar together into soft peaks.

    When chocolate mixture is cool, fold in whipped cream and refrigerate. (May be kept refrigerated for up to 1 week.)

Fruit Sauces

(all sauces are made the same)

$1^1\!/_2$ **cups fresh fruit**

$^1\!/_2$ **cup confectioners' sugar**

1 ounce corresponding fruit flavored liqueur

   (schnapps, Chambord, etc.)

    Purée fruit (for peaches, peel first), sugar and liqueur in a blender. Remove and strain. Refrigerate until ready to use. Repeat recipe to make 3 different fruit sauces. (Sauces may be made up to 2 days in advance.)

✶ Todd Brown

Brewer's East Inn, VA Beach

A man who has traveled around the globe, Chef Todd Brown didn't need to look further than his own backyard to find his professional calling. Growing up on a farm, Chef Brown learned the art of cultivating, handling, cooking and serving food. "Learning how to cook food is one thing, but being passionate about it is another. I have my mom to thank for that." Todd's French and German heritage as well as his voyages as a Merchant Marines has influenced the menu at Brewer's East Inn.

A marital coalescence of the Brewer and Brown families opened the way for a "yours, mine and ours" business phenomenon resulting in enough business partners to corner many markets. The Brewer's East Inn is just one part of Family Ventures, LC, headed by all 11 children of the Brewer-Brown clan: Amy, Dusty, Gigi, John, Laura, Matthew, Megan, Robby, Scott, Susan and Todd.

Chef Brown earned his degree at the Culinary Arts Institute of Baltimore, and has spent most of his career working in Virginia, Maryland and New York. An assortment of awards garnish his resume, including second place in the Crab Cooking Olympics (1985), Outstanding Young Man of America (1987), best in show at the WNIS Power Party (1995), first place at the Great California Cuisine Cook-

Off (1995), and first place at the Gourmet Gala (1995). He can be heard speaking about various topics of specialization within the culinary profession. Chef Brown can periodically be seen showing off his talents on WAVY, TV10's *The Great Chefs of Hampton Roads* with live cooking demonstrations.

Even with his busy schedule, Chef Brown takes time to indulge in his favorite hobby, his garden. This hobby proves both profitable and therapeutic. Many of the fresh fruits and vegetables served at the Brewer's East Inn are grown on the premises.

"One of my favorite times of the day is to leave the hustle and bustle of the restaurant and relax picking vegetables in the garden behind the restaurant. It's very rewarding to grow, harvest, prepare and serve a vegetable and to know my customers are getting the freshest product available. It just can't get any better than that."

Success came quickly for the Brewer's East Inn. "I think it is because we serve good, wholesome food in a consistent manner with flair." Organization is another component in Chef Brown's formula for success. "The more organized you are, coupled with talented help, the more time you have to create new and exciting dishes."

You'll feel like part of the family dining

on Pennsylvania Dutch family-style meals in a relaxed atmosphere after being greeted at the door and served by a Brewer/Brown family member. A selection from the á la carte menu will lead you to a sampling of Chef Brown's cross-cultural cuisine. "I read just about anything food-oriented I can get my hands on. It keeps me up-to-date on new food trends – it keeps me in check."

Chef Brown grew up cooking for a crowd, and his basic advice is easy to follow – reduce the stress! "Everyone will enjoy themselves, and in a stress-free environment you'll be able to do your best creating and cooking."

Pan-Seared Sea Bass over Barbecue Lentils with Rhubarb and Wild Berry Chutney

1/4 cup sesame oil

2 (6 ounce) sea bass fillets

salt and pepper to taste

1 teaspoon curry powder

1 pound rhubarb, sliced

1/4 cup sliced red onion

1/4 cup sliced scallions

1/4 cup sliced red bell pepper

1/3 cup wild berry schnapps

1/4 cup chicken stock

1 1/2 cups fresh Crenshaw melon, small dice

1/3 cup raspberry or blackberry sauce

2/3 cup Major Grey's Chutney

1 pint mixed wild berries

Barbecue lentils, 2 servings
   (lentils cooked in barbecue sauce)

Garnish: fresh herbs

Heat sesame oil in a large skillet. Season bass fillets with salt, pepper and half of curry powder.

Sear bass in skillet for 30 seconds on one side and 1 minute on the other. Remove fillets from skillet.

Add rhubarb, red onion, scallions, red pepper and remainder of curry powder to skillet. Sauté for 1 minute. Add wild berry schnapps and flambé until fire dies down. (**CAUTION:** *Remove skillet from stove before adding schnapps.*) Add chicken stock and reduce by 1/3. Add melon and berry sauce, stir in chutney, then reduce heat and add fresh berries. Return fillets to the skillet. Reheat thoroughly.

Place barbecue lentils on plate then place bass fillet on lentils. Ladle sauce over fillet, garnish and serve. Repeat for second serving. **Serves 2**

Chef's Note: If Crenshaw melon is not available, substitute cantaloupe melon.

Warm Tomato-Cucumber Relish

2/3 cup extra virgin olive oil

1/2 cup balsamic vinegar

1 teaspoon salt

1 tablespoon cracked black pepper

1/3 cup coarsely chopped parsley

1 clove garlic, minced

1 tablespoon sugar

2 (28 ounce) cans whole peeled tomatoes,
   drained, large dice

1 medium red onion, sliced into thin strips

3 large cucumbers, skinned, seeded,
   cut into 1/2" slices

In a large stainless-steel bowl, combine olive oil, vinegar, salt, pepper, parsley, garlic and sugar. Whip together to combine. Add tomatoes, onion and cucumbers.

Heat a large sauté pan over medium temperature. Sauté mixture for 5 minutes (do not over cook). This mixture can be made ahead of time and stored in the refrigerator and heated before use.

Chef's Note: Serve over your favorite cooked fish.

Pan-Roasted Lean Generation Pork Medallions over Italian Sauté

3 medium red-skinned potatoes, steamed, cooled,
    cut in 1" cubes
oil for deep frying potatoes
1/3 cup olive oil
4 (4 ounce) Lean Generation pork loin medallions
salt and pepper to taste
3 garlic cloves, roasted
4 scallions, cut into 1" pieces
1/2 cup cherry peppers, cut in half
1 cup portobello mushrooms, cut in half,
    sliced in 1" pieces
3 sprigs fresh oregano
salt and coarse ground black pepper to taste
1/4 cup Galliano liqueur
1 tablespoon balsamic vinegar
Garnish: fresh herbs

Deep fry potatoes until golden brown. Drain oil from potatoes and set aside.

Preheat oven to 325°.

Heat a large sauté pan over medium-high temperature and add olive oil. Season pork medallions with salt and pepper. Sear in pan for 2 minutes on each side. Remove medallions from pan to an ovenproof dish. Bake pork medallions in oven until desired degree of doneness is achieved.

Add roasted garlic cloves, scallions, peppers and mushrooms to the sauté pan. Sauté for 1 minute. Add deep fried potatoes, whole sprigs of oregano, salt and pepper and sauté for 30 seconds more.

Add Galliano and flambé. (**CAUTION**: *remove pan from stove before adding Galliano*) After fire dies, return to stove and add balsamic vinegar. Cook for 30 seconds more and turn off heat. Transfer vegetable mixture onto a plate with a slotted spoon.

Take medallions out of oven and place on vegetables. Pour liquid from sauté pan over medallions. Garnish with fresh herbs. **Serves 4**

Black Bean Salsa

1 1/2 cups cooked black beans, cooled and drained
1 teaspoon ground cumin
2 small cans diced green chilies
2 cups chunky salsa
1/2 cup red wine vinegar
1/2 cup hoisin sauce
1 bunch scallions, sliced thin
1/4 cup finely chopped cilantro
1 serrano pepper, seeded and minced
1 small red onion, small dice
3 tablespoons lime juice

Place all ingredients in a heavy-bottomed pot and mix well. Heat over medium temperature, stirring occasionally. Bring to a simmer and remove from heat. Cool completely and transfer to a non-metal container and store in refrigerator until ready to use.

Chef's Note: If using canned black beans, be sure to rinse well.

Chicken Gecko

2 (6 ounce) boneless, skinless chicken breasts

¼ pound andouille sausage, cut lengthwise,
   sliced in ½" pieces

6 medium white mushrooms, cut in quarters

4 scallions, sliced into ½" pieces

1 clove garlic, minced

1 red bell pepper, medium dice

¼ cup olive oil

1 tablespoon butter

1 tablespoon Cajun seasoning

6 large fresh basil leaves, chopped fine

1 cup bronzing mixture (recipe to follow)

roasted pecan wild rice pilaf (recipe to follow)

½ cup hollandaise sauce (recipe to follow)

Preheat grill.

Dip chicken in Bronzing Mixture. Grill for 4 minutes on each side or until done.

In a large pan over high temperature, sauté sausage, mushrooms, scallions, garlic and pepper in olive oil and butter. Add Cajun seasoning.

To assemble on a serving plate, place chicken on top of Roasted Pecan Wild Rice Pilaf. Top chicken with andouille mixture. Top all with Hollandaise Sauce. **Serves 2**

Bronzing Mixture

½ cup Cajun seasoning

2 tablespoons dark brown sugar

½ cup salad oil

Mix all ingredients together. Consistency should be like wet sand.

Roasted Pecan Wild Rice Pilaf

1 box Uncle Ben's Wild Rice Pilaf

1 cup roasted pecans, chopped fine

Preheat oven to 375°. Cook wild rice pilaf following package directions.

Roast pecans in oven for 5 minutes. Chop and add to pilaf while both are still hot. Cover to incorporate aromas.

Hollandaise Sauce

3 egg yolks

½ tablespoon water

12 ounces clarified butter

2 tablespoons lemon juice

pinch of salt

3 drops Tabasco Sauce

2 drops Worcestershire Sauce

Place egg yolks in a stainless-steel bowl. Add water. Place bowl over a pot of boiling water. Whip yolks vigorously until they turn a very pale yellow and double in volume. Remove from heat.

Very slowly, while constantly whipping, add clarified butter and lemon juice alternately and in small amounts. Add Tabasco, Worcestershire and salt. Whip to incorporate.

Hold hollandaise near enough to heat to keep warm, but not too close. (High heat will cause the sauce to break down.)

Chef's Note: Hollandaise may not be held longer than 3 hours.

Monroe Duncan
Chef and Food Service Consultant

Chef Monroe Duncan neither aspired to celebrity chef status nor thought his culinary rudiments enough to warrant professional recognition, yet his career spans almost four decades and he has firmly established himself as the culinary patriarch of Hampton Roads. He lays claim to the first open kitchen in the first chef-owned restaurant in the area, and he continues to serve innovative and regional cuisine to his customers. His culinary prowess was forged in the 60s and 70s by formidable apprenticeships with the industry's best, while he pursued a cursory education in English literature.

"It was my mother's inspiration that enticed me into this cooking lunacy when I was literally tied to her apron strings!" Monroe Duncan's mother, Blossom, whipped up some scrumptious victuals at her mother's farm in Oswego, South Carolina, when he was knee-high to a grasshopper. Monroe recalls wonderful cold and misty mornings when both his mother and his Grandmother would prance around an old wood-burning stove serving up fried eggs, country ham, redeye gravy, grits, and the best biscuits life has to offer, all accompanied by Grandma Ida's grand home-made fig preserves.

Needless to say, his cookery, "part buffoonery and part know-how, is fraught with Mama's magic touch." Indeed Chef Duncan's food is magic. It's his nirvana, and it will be your heaven, too. "I would never serve anything I don't like. I'm lucky to have very educated taste buds, and lucky to have customers that agree with me!"

His menu diversity has evolved from a standard bill-of-fare at Suddenly Last Summer, to his latest culinary renditions found at Phantoms Catering. His extraordinary creations are sought after by many and make there way onto menus throughout the Tidewater area. Chef Duncan's success gives new meaning to the phrase, "You've come a long way baby!"

"Cooking isn't really difficult, but you have to practice the art of it and wear your heart on every plate that leaves your kitchen." Chef Duncan says the perfect balance comes from harmoniously performing for receptive taste buds. Tripping the light fantastic with patrons is the answer, the reward, the prize.

Wherever Chef Duncan dons his toque (or ties a rag around his brow) and puts hand to pan, his culinary fans are sure to follow. The mystique of his reputation beckons patrons from all over the Tidewater area and beyond. A select coterie of chefs and food service professionals are among his admirers and protégés, and many have completed their culinary school apprenticeships under his inspired tutelage. "These students are the jewels in my toque, the joy of my career and the fruition of my future."

On the cutting edge of gourmet passions, Monroe's trend-setting cookery delivers ambrosia to his family of customers. "I have seen generations of regular customers in my establishments over the years, and I will create and cook for their progeny."

Seafood Lasagna with Brandied-Basil Cream Sauce

Seafood Lasagna

8 cups ricotta cheese

1½ cups grated Parmesan cheese

¾ pound provolone cheese, shredded

6 eggs

24 fresh basil leaves, chopped

1 tablespoon black pepper

1 pound lasagna noodles, cooked

**24 large shrimp, peeled, deveined
  and cut lengthwise**

1 pound lump crabmeat, picked over

2 pounds sea scallops, large dice

9 thin slices of provolone cheese

Brandied-Basil Cream Sauce (recipe to follow)

Garnish: fresh basil leaves

Preheat oven to 350°. This recipe should make 3 layers.

In a bowl, mix together ricotta, Parmesan, shredded provolone, eggs, basil and black pepper.

Spray the bottom of a lasagna pan with a cooking spray. Add a layer of noodles. Spread a thin layer of cheese mixture to cover noodle layer and top with a layer of shrimp, crabmeat and scallops. Repeat steps again, ending with a layer of noodles until you have completed the process 3 times.

Arrange provolone cheese slices on top of lasagna. Bake for approximately 1 hour or until golden brown and bubbly.

To serve, cut into portions and place lasagna on a plate. Generously spoon Brandied-Basil Cream Sauce over the top and garnish with fresh basil. **Serves 9-12**

Chef's Note: This lasagna recipe is also good with a marinara sauce accompanying the Brandied-Basil Cream Sauce.

This recipe can be converted easily for fewer portions. This lasagna does not freeze well because the cheese mixture has a tendency to break down. If there are any leftovers, refrigerate and microwave when ready to serve.

Brandied-Basil Cream Sauce

2 cups heavy cream

½ cup cognac or brandy

12 fresh basil leaves, chopped

1 cup shrimp stock

½ cup grated Parmesan cheese

salt and white pepper to taste

Bring heavy cream, cognac, basil leaves and stock to a boil. Reduce mixture to preferred consistency. Add Parmesan cheese, stirring to melt, and remove from heat.

Chef's Note: Use Minor's shrimp base to make the shrimp stock, or make your own shrimp stock by boiling together and reducing by ⅔ the following ingredients: shells from 5 pounds of shrimp, 1 peeled Bermuda onion studded with 8 whole cloves, 3 bay leaves, 2 tablespoons whole black peppercorns, and 5 quarts of water.

Panéed Shad Roe on Dandelion Greens with White Asparagus, Wild Onion and Bacon Bercy

1 pound fresh blanched white asparagus

salt

¾ cup corn oil

4 (6-8 ounce) pairs of shad roe

2 cups of seasoned flour for dredging

4 handfuls fresh dandelion greens

8 ounces lightly salted butter

2 teaspoons chopped parsley

3 tablespoons chopped, crisp bacon

3 tablespoons chopped wild onions

¾ cup dry white wine

3 teaspoons freshly squeezed lemon juice

Blanch asparagus in boiling salted water for 3-4 minutes, and then shock in ice cold water to stop the cooking process.

Add corn oil to a large skillet, preferably cast iron. Lightly dredge shad roe in seasoned flour and carefully shake off excess flour. When the oil is hot, gently place the roe into the skillet and brown on both sides until the edges are crisp. Remove from pan and keep warm.

Toss the dandelion leaves into the remaining hot oil. Sauté the leaves, separating them so that each will become crisp, being careful not to burn. Remove from skillet and drain on paper towels.

Arrange dandelion greens into four neat nests on a serving platter. Place one pair of shad roe onto each of the nests. Keep warm.

Discard the remaining oil from the skillet. Add butter and melt. Add the blanched asparagus and sauté for about 3 minutes being careful not to burn the butter. Add the parsley, crisp bacon and wild onions. Sauté for 1 minute. Add the wine and reduce until the sauce becomes creamy. Add lemon juice.

Arrange equal portions of asparagus between each set of shad roe lobes. Pour sauce over and serve immediately. **Serves 4**

Parsleyed Potatoes with Fresh Mint

12 small new potatoes, either peeled, unpeeled or pattern peeled

4 ounces melted butter

2 tablespoons chopped parsley

1 tablespoon chopped fresh mint

Boil potatoes until soft. Toss them in the melted butter, chopped parsley and chopped mint. **Serves 4**

Sautéed Fillet of Norwegian Salmon with Fresh Basil Pecan Meunière

½ cup corn oil

6 (6 ounce) salmon fillets, pin bones removed

seasoned flour for dredging

6 ounces lightly salted butter

juice of 1 lemon

1 cup pecan pieces

18 large fresh basil leaves

Heat corn oil in large skillet or sauté pan.

Lightly dredge salmon fillets in flour. Shake off excess flour. Place skinside down in pan and sauté until brown on both sides, being careful not to overcook. Remove the fillets from the pan and keep hot.

Pour off cooking oil. Add butter to the pan. Place basil leaves in melting butter. The leaves will begin to crisp. Sauté them until they are brittle and the butter is brown, but not burnt. Add the pecans and lemon juice. Place fillet on plate and top with meunière and serve immediately while the butter is still foaming. **Serves 6**

Thomas Evaldi

Gus' Mariner Restaurant, VA Beach

Fresh seafood takes center stage at Gus' Mariner Restaurant, where Thomas Evaldi is the behind-the-scenes Executive Chef. "Just let the food do the talking" is his principle, and his award-winning recipes speak for themselves. When he isn't creating delectable delights in the kitchen, he is running the 175-seat restaurant and its five banquet and private dining rooms.

Beginning his career as a short-order cook at the local drug store in St. Petersburg, Florida, Chef Evaldi knew cooking was his calling and saved his money so he could attend the Culinary Institute of America in New York. After graduating from the Institute, Chef Evaldi came to Virginia Beach to attend the wedding of his college roommate, Gordon Christie. He enjoyed the area so much that he decided to stay and became Executive Chef at the Lynnhaven Fish House.

In 1982, Chef Evaldi and Gus Mengulus opened Gus' Fish House at the Ramada Inn, Virginia Beach, changing its name in 1984 to Gus' Mariner Restaurant. They broadened the menu and the client base, resulting in a gross of over $2.5 million annually on food and beverages. Customers are always eager to feast on the award-winning cuisine of Chef Evaldi. He was named "Chef of the Year" by the Tidewater Chef's Association in 1988. He has

also earned a Golden Fork Award every year since 1988, the National Ramada Inn Food and Beverage Award in 1989, and was first finalist for the award in 1990, 1991, and 1995.

Chef Evaldi sums up his formula for success in one word: consistency! "I also have a great deal of pride in this restaurant because I helped open it. Everyone who works here shares in this pride and presents quality work." The location is a definite plus. Oceanside ambience abounds, granting diners a glimpse of dolphins playing in the summer and whales swimming by in the winter.

Chef Evaldi works very hard at creating a well-rounded menu while keeping his prices as low as possible. "People like to eat out as often as their budgets will allow. We have to stay competitive with the places around us that deliver, and we want to be family-friendly. It's very hard to take a family out to dinner and experience a quality evening without spending an arm and a leg." Gus' offers early-bird specials and The Pub offers casual dining.

"Less is more" is the motto Chef Evaldi lives by in the kitchen. "Keep it simple. Use the goodness of the food products to make your dish a success." Part of Chef Evaldi's success is his staff, to which he gives much of the acclaim. Many of the same employees

have been with him for a very long time. "This is how standards can be set and trust is built." He credits his ability to stay with the newest trends to the local talent graduating from Johnson & Wales University in Norfolk. "Having a culinary arts school in the area keeps food in the forefront of everyone's mind, and that keeps restaurants on their toes."

Chef Evaldi resides in Virginia Beach. He has two children, Becky and Brian. When he is not spending time with his family, he's probably either fishing, exercising at the gym, or bike riding.

Gus' offers plenty of parking, which many establishments along the oceanfront can't boast. The Ramada Inn welcomes special banquets and parties and will individualize menus for all occasions. "We'll do anything to make our customers happy because we want them to come back."

Tortellini and Seafood Salad with Tarragon Vinaigrette Dressing

Tortellini and Seafood Salad

Tarragon Vinaigrette Dressing (recipe to follow)
$1/2$ pound cheese tortellini
$1/2$ pound spinach tortellini
$1/2$ pound bay scallops
$1/2$ pound small shrimp
4 ounces artichoke hearts, chopped
$1/2$ cup chopped red pepper
4 scallions, chopped

Make Tarragon Vinaigrette Dressing and set aside.

Boil tortellini until tender. Drain and cool. Poach the shrimp and scallops until done. Drain and cool. Combine all salad ingredients together. Pour dressing over salad and marinate overnight. **Serves 4**

Tarragon Vinaigrette Dressing

$1/2$ cup cider vinegar
1 tablespoon tarragon
1 teaspoon salt
1 tablespoon Dijon mustard
2 teaspoons sugar
1 garlic clove, minced
dash of white pepper
$1^1/4$ cups vegetable oil

Combine all ingredients and mix well.

Fillet of Flounder Meunière

1 fresh fillet of flounder, all bones removed
seasoned flour for dredging
egg wash
1 cup fresh bread crumbs
$1/4$ cup chopped parsley
clarified butter for sautéing
oil for sautéing
3 pats butter, softened
juice of $1/2$ lemon

Split the flounder down the middle and remove the skin with a sharp knife.

Dredge the skinless flounder in the seasoned flour, then in the egg wash, and then in the bread crumbs mixed with half of parsley.

Sauté the breaded flounder to a golden brown in a 50/50 mixture of clarified butter and oil. Remove from the pan to a serving platter.

Place a small sauté pan over high temperature. When pan is hot add the softened butter. Allow the butter to bubble and brown, but do not burn. When the butter is browned squeeze in lemon and add remaining chopped parsley. Pour butter and lemon mixture over the sautéed fish and serve immediately. **Serves 2**

Scallop and Crabmeat Sea Cakes with Black Bean Relish

1 pound fresh backfin crabmeat

margarine for sautéing

½ pound raw sea scallops

1 tablespoon heavy cream

2 teaspoons chopped cilantro

pinch of salt

dash of white pepper

2 tablespoons chopped carrots

1 tablespoon chopped green onion

2 tablespoons chopped red bell pepper

½ cup milk mixed with ⅓ cup flour

2 tablespoons Dijon mustard

2 tablespoons melted butter

1 tablespoon Lea & Perrins White Wine
  Worcestershire Sauce

1 egg yolk

1 egg

Black Bean Relish (recipe to follow)

Place all ingredients except crabmeat and margarine into a food processor. Purée and pour into a chilled stainless-steel bowl. The ingredients must remain cold while you work with them (see Chef's Note). Add the crabmeat and fold in carefully.

Heat a skillet and add margarine. Portion the mixture with a large ice cream scoop onto the hot skillet. Sauté until golden brown on each side.

Place the cakes on a nest of Black Bean Relish and serve with your favorite vegetable. **Serves 4**

Chef's Note: The best way to keep the ingredients cold is to chill the bowl by setting it on top of a bowl of ice while you work. Before cooking crab cake, chill thoroughly – overnight if possible.

Crab cake batter is runny and should be cooked in the same manner as you would a pancake.

Black Bean Relish

1 pound dry black beans

2 quarts cold water

¼ cup olive oil

1 teaspoon minced garlic

1 cup diced onion

½ cup diced red bell pepper

1 cup whole kernel corn

1 cup diced canned tomatoes

½ cup cider vinegar

2 tablespoons brown sugar

1 pint beer

1 tablespoon salt

1 cup diced green chili peppers

2 teaspoons ground cumin

Drain and rinse the black beans. Place in a pot with water. Bring to a boil. Reduce heat and simmer until tender.

In a separate pot, sauté garlic, onion and pepper in olive oil until onions are transparent. Add the remaining ingredients and simmer approximately 15 minutes.

Combine the vegetable mixture with the black beans and simmer until the beans reduce down and the liquid is thickened. Serve warm.

Mom's Lasagna

Parmesan or Romano cheese

Thin slices of mozzarella cheese

Preheat oven to 300°.

To assemble lasagna, cover the bottom of a baking pan with Tomato Sauce (recipe to follow), then cover with a layer of Home-Made Lasagna Noodles (recipe to follow). Cover this with a layer of Spinach/Meat Mixture (recipe to follow), then another layer of noodles. Next add the Ricotta Cheese Mixture (recipe to follow) and cover with another layer of noodles. Pour remaining sauce over all layers as needed, being sure to let it run down the sides of the casserole inside the pan. Sprinkle with Parmesan or Romano cheese and cover with thin slices of mozzarella cheese.

Bake in oven until sauce is bubbly and cheese browns, approximately 2 hours. **Serves 8**

Tomato Sauce

1 pound Italian sausage

2 pork chops

1/3 cup olive or vegetable oil

1/2 cup chopped onion

2-3 cloves garlic, crushed

1 (28 ounce) can tomato purée

2 (28 ounce) cans tomatoes

1 can (6 ounces) tomato paste

1 package Lawry's spaghetti sauce mix

1 tablespoon Italian seasoning

1 tablespoon sugar

1 tablespoon salt

1/2 teaspoon pepper

1/2 cup grated Parmesan or Romano cheese

water as needed

tomato paste as needed

In a large pot, brown meat in oil. Add onions and garlic. Simmer until tender, but not brown. Add remaining ingredients. Bring to a boil, then simmer on low heat for several hours until meat is tender and flavors are blended. Add water or tomato paste as needed for desired consistency.

Home-Made Lasagna Noodles

4 eggs

2 tablespoons water

1 teaspoon olive oil

1/2 teaspoon salt

1 3/4-2 cups unsifted, all-purpose flour

1 tablespoon vegetable oil

salt

Beat together the eggs, water, oil and salt just until blended. Spoon 1 1/2 cups of flour into a large mixing bowl and make a cavity in the center. Pour in the egg mixture and stir until the flour is well moistened. Press into a ball.

Sprinkle the remaining flour on a board or pastry cloth and knead until very smooth and elastic, about 10 minutes. Chill 1 hour.

Divide the dough into equal portions and roll out as thin as possible. Cut into strips approximately 3 inches wide. Spread out on lightly floured sheets of wax paper until ready to cook.

Add oil to a large pot of salted water. Boil pasta uncovered for 2-3 minutes or until done. Pour into a colander and rinse with cold water.

Chef's Note: Store-bought noodles may be substituted for above recipe.

(Continued on next page.)

Spinach/Meat Mixture

½ cup Italian bread crumbs

1 package frozen chopped spinach

1 (8 ounce) can mushroom stems and pieces

1 egg, beaten

2 tablespoons Parmesan cheese

1½ pounds ground meat, browned (beef, pork,
*   Italian sausage or a combination)*

1 clove garlic, minced

salt and pepper to taste

Combine all ingredients and mix well.

Ricotta Cheese Mixture

2 pounds ricotta cheese

½ pound mozzarella cheese, diced

¼ cup grated Parmesan or Romano cheese

1 tablespoon chopped parsley

2 eggs, beaten

¼ teaspoon pepper

1 teaspoon salt

¼ teaspoon nutmeg

Combine all ingredients and mix well.

Dolphin with Christo Sauce

Christo Sauce (recipe to follow)

4 (8-10 ounce) fillets of fresh dolphin

melted butter for basting

juice of 1 lemon

Old Bay Seasoning

Prepare Christo Sauce and keep warm.
Preheat oven to 450°.
Place dolphin fillets on a sheet pan and baste with butter. Squeeze the fresh lemon over the fillets and sprinkle lightly with Old Bay Seasoning. Place the fillets in oven and bake until firm to touch, approximately 10-15 minutes.
Spoon Christo Sauce over the baked dolphin and serve immediately. **Serves 4**

Christo Sauce

4 ounces butter

2 teaspoons minced garlic

2 fresh tomatoes, diced

1 (14 ounce) can artichoke hearts, large chop

1 cup fresh chopped mushrooms

4 tablespoons capers

2 tablespoons chopped fresh parsley

1 cup dry white wine

Place a sauté pan on stove over high temperature. Add butter and melt. Add the garlic and sauté until garlic becomes tan in color. Add the tomatoes, artichoke hearts, mushrooms, capers and chopped parsley. Sauté until all vegetables are heated thoroughly. Add the white wine and reduce until the sauce slightly thickens. (**CAUTION:** *Remove pan from stove before adding wine.*)

Patrick Galiardi

Sages, VA Beach

Chef Patrick Galiardi polished his skills at a variety of trendy dining spots in the Tidewater area – Locks Pointe, Le Chambord, The Lucky Star, Boogies, Coastal Grill, The Coyote Cafe, Cafe Society, The Cavalier Golf and Yacht Club and Bistro 210 – before opening Sages in Virginia Beach. Most chefs credit "dear old mom" with their passion for cooking, but Chef Galiardi declares his passion came from his father. "He can put anything together. He taught me that every type of food has endless possibilities." A family heritage rich in French and Italian ethnic food values taught Chef Galiardi to pay attention to details – to dissect food down to its basic elements.

Labeling himself as a traditional chef, Patrick insists on treating food with the utmost respect. "I tend not to get wild with food. You've got to do things basically and put foods together in a tasteful and simple manner." Spending time in New England taught Patrick a lot about cooking, too. "Northern chefs have a strong sense of food, especially about what is considered right and wrong." Love for good eating and a desire for self-satisfaction are what led Patrick in the direction of opening up his own restaurant, along with a hunger to act upon the Provençal influences tugging at his soul.

At Sages, you'll notice periodic changes on the menu, which reflect Chef Galiardi's desire to bring the seasons inside his restaurant. He also aspires to bring the level of dining in the Tidewater area up a notch by using the region's best products.

Chef Galiardi's advice to the home gourmet: "Fall in love with cooking! Get into it! Don't make cooking a chore. If you develop a passion for cooking, you'll thirst for all the knowledge you can get about food. The more you understand, the more sense everything will make."

Because Patrick tries try to appeal to a variety of diners, you'll find a little of everything on the menu at Sages. "I'll work really hard to get the chicken lover to love my chicken!" He wants his customers to begin their evening with great excitement and anticipation about eating at Sages, and he makes sure that they leave with their expectations fulfilled. "I think people are tired of not getting their money's worth when they eat out. Personally, I'd prefer to eat at a modest-style establishment and get blown away by the food, rather than eat at a notorious establishment and experience a just adequate meal. I'm looking for something outstanding. I hope my customers are too."

Patrick is a hands-on chef and is usually at the restaurant cooking, so he doesn't get a lot of free time for relaxation. When he does get away, he heads straight for the great outdoors and enjoys partaking in a variety of sporting activities. "When I feel comfortable about Sages, I might consider opening another restaurant, something with a different theme, but I'll definitely stay in the Tidewater area."

With a wealth of talented chefs in the area, Chef Galiardi knows he has to aim high to please his customers. "I'm a very humble person. I don't know if I'm successful yet, but I definitely know that I have the desire to cook food, and I definitely have the energy to do it all!"

White Flageolet and Prosciutto Soup

2 pounds cannellini beans

1 large onion, small dice

10 cloves garlic, chopped fine

3 cups julienne prosciutto

3 tablespoons extra virgin olive oil

⅛ cup rosemary, fine chop

1½ gallons good quality chicken stock

⅛ cup sea salt

8 cups fresh spinach, washed, cut
*   into 1" strips*

2 cups sun-dried tomatoes, julienne

6 cups grated Parmesan cheese

Sift through beans and discard any pebbles. In a large pot, soak beans in water for 3 hours. Drain. Add onion, garlic, prosciutto and olive oil. Sauté until onions are translucent. Add rosemary, chicken stock and sea salt. Simmer for 45-60 minutes. When beans are tender, stir in spinach and sun-dried tomatoes. Season with sea salt to taste.

Preheat oven to 400°. Spread Parmesan cheese onto a flat pan. Place in oven to bake. When it is finished, it will look like a large cheese chip. (Be very careful: this process doesn't take long.) When cool, break a serving off and serve on the side with the soup. **Serves 8**

Roasted Chicken with Wild Mushroom Ragoût

2 (2½ pound) chickens, whole

½ cup dried thyme

½ cup dried oregano

¾ cup sea salt

2 whole heads garlic, crushed

6 bay leaves

8 ounces unsalted butter, softened

peanut oil for coating pan

4 tablespoons peanut oil

3 cups shiitake mushrooms, large chop

3 cups oyster mushrooms, large chop

1 cup finely diced shallots

½ cup fresh tarragon, rough chop

2 cups Madeira wine

2 cups demi-glace

1 tablespoon butter

trussing string

sea salt to taste

Preheat oven to 475°.

Remove the body fat from inside the cavity of the birds.

Mix thyme, oregano and sea salt together to create an herb mixture. Place one head of garlic, half of herb mixture, and 3 bay leaves inside each chicken. With your hand covering the cavity so the mix does not spill out, shake the chickens to ensure the cavity is well coated.

On a flat, sturdy surface truss the chickens in a traditional style, neck facing you, folding the wings under the body. Rub the entire outside of chickens with softened butter, coating well.

(Continued on next page)

Coat a sheet pan with peanut oil and place in oven. When oil starts to smoke lightly, place the chickens in the oven, breast side down, with cavity facing out. Roast for 20 minutes and turn over. Reduce heat to 375° and cook for 25 minutes. When nicely browned and desired degree of doneness is achieved, remove chickens from oven and let rest.

Meanwhile, place a large sauté pan on the stove and bring up to temperature. Add 4 tablespoons peanut oil and heat until oil begins to smoke. Add the mushrooms and sauté until lightly browned. Add shallots and tarragon. Sauté for 3-4 minutes, being careful not to burn shallots. Deglaze pan with Madeira and reduce by half. (**CAUTION**: *Remove pan from stove before adding wine.*) Add the demi-glace and reduce by half. Add butter to thicken sauce and season with sea salt to taste.
Serves 4

Atlantic Salmon with Garlic, Horseradish, Japanese Bread Crumbs and Caper Sauce

4 (6 ounce) salmon fillets, skinned, pin bones removed
1/2 cup ground horseradish
1/4 cup finely chopped garlic
Japanese bread crumbs*
3 tablespoons peanut oil

Preheat oven to 350°.
Mix horseradish and garlic together. Gently rub horseradish/garlic mixture on salmon fillets, coating evenly.
Roll salmon in Japanese bread crumbs. Place a sauté pan over medium temperature. Add peanut oil and bring it up to pan temperature. Place salmon fillets in pan and sauté until brown. Turn fillets over and place in oven for 4-5 minutes.

*Chef's Note: Japanese bread crumbs, also known as panko, are coarser than those normally used in the United States and create a crunchy crust. They can be found in Asian markets.

Caper Sauce

1/2 cup kalamata olives, pitted
1/2 cup sun-dried tomatoes, julienne
1/2 cup capers, chopped
1/2 cup leeks, julienne
1/4 cup dry vermouth
1/2 cup chicken stock
1 tablespoon unsalted butter
sea salt to taste

Sauté olives, sun-dried tomatoes, capers, and leeks over high temperature. After 30 seconds, deglaze with vermouth and reduce by half. (**CAUTION:** *remove pan from stove before adding vermouth.*) Add chicken stock and reduce by 1/3. Add butter to thicken sauce. Season with sea salt. **Serves 4**

Pan-Roasted Squab with Black Olive Polenta

4 fresh or frozen squabs

2 cups olive oil

½ bunch fresh thyme

½ bunch fresh rosemary

1 head of garlic, chopped

1 tablespoon fresh ground black pepper

Black Olive Polenta (recipe to follow)

Squab Stock (recipe to follow)

Red Pepper Purée (recipe to follow)

Preheat oven to 350°.

While keeping intact, de-bone breast and leg sections of squabs, reserving the bones for stock. Place squabs in a large pan along with herbs, garlic, olive oil and black pepper. Marinate for at least 4 hours.

Sear squabs in a hot, ovenproof skillet, skin side down. When browned, place in oven for approximately 25 minutes or until desired degree of doneness is achieved.

To serve, place the Black Olive Polenta on a serving plate. Remove the breast from the leg and slice. Place on top of the polenta and arrange the legs. Sauce the plate with squab stock and roasted red pepper purée. **Serves 4**

Black Olive Polenta

16 cups water

8 cups yellow cornmeal

2 cups kalamata olives, pitted, rough chop

sea salt

4 ounces unsalted butter

Bring water to a boil and slowly whisk in cornmeal. (Mixture should start to get thick.) Add the olives and butter. Season with sea salt to taste. Cover and set aside. Reheat thoroughly before serving.

Squab Stock

reserved bones from squabs

1 carrot, rough chop

1 onion, rough chop

1 stalk of celery, rough chop

1 gallon water

1 bay leaf

½ bottle (750 ml) red wine

Preheat oven to 350°. Roast squab bones, carrot, onion and celery in oven until browned. Deglaze pan with red wine. **(CAUTION:** *Remove pan from heat source before adding wine).*

Transfer stock ingredients to a pot and add 1 gallon of water plus the bay leaf. Let simmer and reduce to a thick consistency. Set aside.

Red Pepper Purée

2 roasted red bell peppers, skinned, seeded

oil to coat peppers

1 tablespoon olive oil to purée with peppers

Preheat oven to 350°. Coat red peppers evenly in oil and roast in oven until blistered. Purée the roasted red peppers along with olive oil until smooth.

Mike Hall

Bienville Grill, Norfolk

Stacey Haines

Chef Mike Hall has come a long way from his first job as pot washer at Geneva General Hospital in New York. "Actually, that's where my interest in cooking started. Every Thursday was grilled steak night. They let me go outside and tend to the grill. I thought that was just the best!" In 1976, Chef Hall graduated from The Rochester Institute of Technology with a degree in Hotel and Restaurant Management. While on a trip to New Orleans with his roommate, Chef Hall grew fond of the area and decided to stay. His first big break was as a sous chef at Ruffino's in the French Quarter, which soon led to his becoming the Executive Chef. This experience was the stepping stone for Chef Hall's mastery of native Louisiana cooking.

Wanting to further his education, Mike enrolled at The Cordon Bleu in Paris, France. "I had a great time. That was a real education. To sit in a cooking class and watch those chefs do those cooking demonstrations wasn't like being in school – it was like a dream."

Returning to the United States from Paris in 1979, Chef Hall went back to Louisiana and worked with the legendary Paul Prudhomme at Commander's Palace. Chef Hall found himself in the forefront of the "blackening" revolution and was taught by the best. "We would spice the meat, dip it in butter, and grill it. We also did it with chicken, and we were the first to do it with fish."

After Commander's Palace, Chef Hall spent more time cooking in New Orleans at The Marriott, the New Orleans Country Club, and Parker's at Canal Place. "Parker's at Canal Place was my first prestigious job. I was 26 years old and was the Executive Chef at a restaurant that cleared over two million dollars a year. Later, the owner confided to me that after a month, he didn't think I was going to make it. Having the education is one thing, but you have to know how to apply it. Eventually, I got all the kinks worked out and it was a great experience."

In 1983, Chef Hall left Parker's and moved to Lafayette, Louisiana. Up to this point, Chef Hall's experience was with Creole cuisine. "Now I was cooking Cajun – one pot dishes, usually with a roux base, rice, gravy, game, rabbit, crawfish, etc. That's cooking!"

That was the point at which Chef Hall started to visualize the Bienville Grill. After getting his business plan together, Mike set out to look at locations for his restaurant. "I had a lot of help from Joe Hoggard. I held a tasting at The Ship's Cabin for prospective investors. I cooked, I served, and I waited tables. With help from the investors and my family, the Bienville Grill opened."

Having paid his dues in the restaurant business, Chef Hall's interests are now in the test kitchen creating new dishes, generating new menus, and developing foods and spices for production that are indigenous to Louisiana. While approximately 80 percent of the menu at the Bienville Grill is fixed, there is still plenty of room for creativity. "The menu works so well, but I always like to take new things and 'Bienville-ize' them!"

The success of the Bienville Grill is definitely based on the great tasting food. "It's the grilling technique that makes our food taste so good. Most people really enjoy the flavor of my grilled fish. My combination of spices enhance the browning, which is one of the secrets to my flavor. It's unique."

Chicken and Sausage Gumbo

¾ **cup vegetable oil**

1 **cup flour**

8 **cups diced yellow onions**

2 **tablespoons minced garlic**

½ **cup diced celery**

½ **cup diced bell pepper**

1½ **gallons Chicken and Sausage Stock**

    (recipe to follow)

5 **dashes Tabasco Sauce**

½ **tablespoon salt**

1 **bay leaf**

½ **tablespoon white pepper**

2½ **pounds cooked pork sausage, sliced**

    (reserved from stock)

diced meat from 1 fresh cooked chicken

    (reserved from stock)

rice, 12 servings

    Prepare Chicken and Sausage Stock. Keep warm.

    To make a brown roux, heat oil to the smoking point in a small cast iron skillet. Add flour, whipping immediately and continuously.

    Once the roux is chocolate brown in color, add it to a large pot. Add the onions, stirring as you go. Simmer the onions and the roux slowly for about 10 minutes. Add the garlic, celery and bell pepper and simmer for another 10 minutes. Add the stock and bring the gumbo to a boil. Add Tabasco, salt, bay leaf and white pepper.

    Skim any foam that floats to the top and reduce temperature to a high simmer. Simmer like this for 1½ hours adding water to maintain the 1½ gallon level. Add the reserved chicken and sausage. Simmer the gumbo for 30 minutes more. Taste the gumbo and season with salt and pepper. Let cool a few minutes before serving. Serve over rice. **Serves 12**

Chicken and Sausage Stock

1 **fresh chicken, halved**

2½ **pounds pork sausage links**

1 **yellow onion**

½ **carrot**

1 **celery stalk**

1½ **gallons water**

    Boil all ingredients together except sausage. Reduce heat and simmer 2-3 hours or until chicken is tender. Remove chicken and cool. Pick meat, cube and reserve.

    Add the sausage to the stock and boil 30 minutes. Remove sausage, cool and slice. Add water as needed to make 1½ gallons of stock. Defat the stock by skimming, or chill and remove fat from the top.

Oysters Bienville

1½ cups grated Parmesan cheese

2 cups grated Swiss cheese

3-4 dozen oysters, washed, shucked and returned to shell

Prepare Bienville Sauce (recipe to follow) and set aside. Preheat oven to 400°.

Spoon Bienville Sauce over oysters and sprinkle with grated Swiss cheese and top with grated Parmesan cheese. Bake in oven until golden brown. Serve immediately.

Bienville Sauce

¾ cup vegetable oil

1 cup flour

2 ounces lightly salted butter

1 cup minced onion

½ cup minced celery

1 tablespoon minced garlic

4 cups shrimp and chicken stock*

1 pound small peeled shrimp

¼ cup whipping cream

½ teaspoon white pepper

5 dashes Tabasco Sauce

½ tablespoon salt

1 tablespoon minced parsley

1 tablespoon minced green onion

½ pound grated Swiss cheese

1 pound lump crabmeat

To make a blond roux heat oil to the smoking point in a small cast iron skillet. Add flour, whipping immediately and continuously until blond in color. Remove from heat and set aside.

Melt butter in a large saucepan. Add onion, celery and garlic. Simmer for 3-5 minutes. Add the stock and bring to a boil. Add the shrimp and bring the sauce back to a boil. Add the roux with a wire whip. Moving quickly, lower the heat and change to a rubber spatula and add the cream, pepper, Tabasco, salt, parsley, green onion and Swiss cheese. Stir constantly as the sauce will be very thick. Simmer 2-3 minutes, stirring as needed to prevent sticking. Fold in crabmeat. Pour into a wide, shallow pan to cool.

*Chef's Note: To make shrimp and chicken stock, use the same method as making chicken and sausage stock on previous page, substituting shells from 2½ pounds of shrimp for sausage.

Praline Sauce

5 cups sugar

4 cups heavy cream

1 cup water

¾ cup praline liqueur

In a large saucepan over high temperature, heat sugar and water, stirring occasionally, until it starts to boil and turn amber in color. Reduce temperature to medium. Add heavy cream a little at a time, stirring constantly until all of the cream is incorporated. Add the praline liqueur and stir. *(CAUTION: Remove saucepan from stove before adding liqueur.)* If you do not have praline liqueur, any cordial may be substituted.

Chef's Note: Serve warm over or under desserts such as cheesecake, bread pudding, etc.

Remoulade Sauce

2 cups mayonnaise

$\frac{1}{2}$ cup Dijon mustard

$\frac{1}{4}$ cup horseradish

$\frac{1}{2}$ tablespoon black pepper

$\frac{1}{2}$ tablespoon white pepper

1 tablespoon small capers

1 tablespoon Worcestershire Sauce

1 tablespoon caper juice

$\frac{1}{4}$ cup minced yellow onions

$\frac{1}{4}$ cup minced green onion

$\frac{1}{4}$ cup red wine vinegar

juice of $\frac{1}{2}$ lemon

$\frac{1}{4}$ cup minced parsley

1 tablespoon minced garlic

8 dashes Tabasco Sauce

$\frac{1}{4}$ cup ketchup

$\frac{1}{2}$ tablespoon salt

Mix ingredients together thoroughly with a whip and chill.
Makes 1 quart

Corn Maque Choux

8 ears fresh corn

2 ounces butter

1 small onion, diced

1 green bell pepper, diced

1 large tomato, diced

1 teaspoon fresh minced garlic

1 cup chicken stock

1 tablespoon salt

1 teaspoon white pepper

4 dashes Tabasco Sauce

2 tablespoons sugar

Cut corn off cob.

In a large saucepan melt the butter. Add the onion and bell pepper. Simmer 15 minutes or until vegetables are tender. Add corn, tomato, garlic and stock. Simmer 15 minutes more, then add salt, white pepper, Tabasco and sugar. Simmer 5 more minutes and serve.

Philip Haushalter

Open Wide, Norfolk/Phil's Grill, VA Beach

Diffident about his "front of the house" charisma, Chef Haushalter likes to focus his energy on food and its presentation. Phil's first restaurant to appear on the Virginia Beach scene was self-titled, Phil's Grill. "This was meant to be a leisurely paced establishment for surfers to hang out and get some really good food after a vigorous day on the beach."

As luck would have it, Phil's Grill has become one of the hottest places to go for good food, grand portions, exceptional prices and an entertaining atmosphere. "Phil's Grill just took off. I had friends coming in to eat, and I would fix them these incredible meals. It's an open kitchen, so everyone can see food as it is prepared and served. Customers just started saying, 'I want whatever that is!' . . . That's how the menu evolved!"

With the opening of Open Wide in Norfolk, Chef Haushalter has completed his yin yang. "At Open Wide, we're into feeding instead of dining. You have to eat every day, and this is a restaurant you can enjoy on a daily basis. You eat when you're hungry, and you dine to satisfy your culinary desires." The emphasis here is on simplicity. Serving fifty to one hundred customers per shift doesn't leave Chef Haushalter extra time for creating architecturally correct dishes lavished with complicated pan sauces. He simply serves it up and watches his customers eat and enjoy.

After graduating from the Culinary Institute of America in New York in 1989, Philip headed to California to work with Wolfgang Puck at Postrio's. "That was a high volume establishment that only produced superior gourmet products. I met several celebrity West Coast chefs while I was there, and I gained a wealth of enrichment from that experience, but I was anxious to head back to the East Coast and start something in my hometown so I could be near my family."

Operating two restaurants means having to hire a large, diverse staff, so Chef Haushalter is constantly challenged to keep his employees happy and interested in cooking. "I let anyone approach me with food ideas. It's fun to experiment, to try new things and change ingredients around. But you can't stop with just a good idea. You have to take your good idea and keep it practical and adapt it to whomever you're serving. Most important: don't ever give up!" Keeping prices down for the customers is one of Chef Haushalter's primary goals. "I think people enjoy their meal more if they are getting a good value. I use inexpensive, yet quality ingredients and cross-utilize them." Preparation is one of Philip's favorite preoccupations. When you're planning and preparing meals, Chef Haushalter says, "Timing is everything!" The more you

practice the art and science of cooking, the more it becomes second nature to you. Taste the food while you're cooking. Once it gets to the table, it's too late."

If you're at the beach and looking for a bang for your buck, Chef Haushalter promises you'll find it at Phil's Grill. In Norfolk, head to Open Wide, a restaurant named after one of Phil's favorite songs. "It wasn't important to me what to name Open Wide. I could have called it anything: Open Wide, Wide Open, everyone still calls it Phil's, or Phil's in Norfolk. The inside joke is that we're open wide in the morning and wide open at night!" This chef's final words of wisdom: "Eat, drink and never cease to intoxicate yourself with the finer things in life because it's not where you're going, it's where you are right now!"

Appetizer of Spinach Thai Shrimp

2 pounds fresh spinach, washed and stemmed

16 large shrimp, peeled, deveined

¼ cup olive oil

¼ cup soy sauce

1 tablespoon hot red pepper flakes

1 teaspoon fresh minced ginger

2 tablespoons honey

1 carrot, shredded

2 cups shredded cabbage

¼ cup dry roasted peanuts

¼ cup shredded coconut

white rice or Chinese cellophane noodles

Wash spinach thoroughly and set aside.

In a small bowl combine shrimp, oil, soy sauce, red pepper flakes, ginger and honey. Set aside.

In a medium sauté pan or wok over high temperature, add shrimp mixture. Quickly add carrot and cabbage. Stir rapidly. Add peanuts and coconut. Continue to stir fry or sauté until shrimp begins to curl and becomes firm. Remove from heat.

Add spinach and toss.

Serve atop steamed white rice or Chinese cellophane noodles. **Serves 4**

French Country Chicken

4 boneless chicken breasts

salt and pepper

flour for dredging

2 cups quartered mushrooms

2 large carrots, large dice

1 cup pearl onions

4 stalks celery, large dice

1 cup green beans or peas

¼ cup olive oil

½ cup white wine

3 cups rich chicken broth

1 teaspoon fresh tarragon

1 teaspoon fresh chopped parsley

Season chicken breasts liberally with salt and pepper. Dredge in flour.

In a bowl place all vegetables and cover with plastic wrap. Microwave on high until carrot and onion are half cooked (about 3 minutes).

Meanwhile heat olive oil in a large skillet or roasting pan. Add chicken breasts and cook until golden brown (about 3 minutes per side). Add white wine and reduce until dry. **(CAUTION:** *Remove skillet from stove before adding wine.*) Add vegetables, chicken broth and herbs. Cover and simmer over low temperature until chicken is firm and vegetables are done. Do not over cook. **Serves 4**

Chef's Note: If you prefer, sauce may be thickened during the last few minutes of cooking by adding a cornstarch slurry.

Caribbean Jerked Sea Bass with Black Bean Salsa

4 (6 ounce) sea bass fillets
¼ cup Caribbean jerk seasoning*
Black Bean Salsa (recipe to follow)

Coat each fillet lightly in jerk seasoning and set aside.
In a hot sauté pan or cast iron skillet cook fish
approximately 4 minutes on each side or until tender and flaky.
Top each fillet with Black Bean Salsa and serve.

*Chef's Note: Caribbean jerk seasoning may be purchased
commercially.

Black Bean Salsa

¼ cup chopped scallions
1 tomato, chopped
1 green pepper, diced
2 cans black beans
1 cup olive oil
¼ cup red wine vinegar

Combine all ingredients and mix well. Refrigerate until
needed.

Pan-Seared Salmon with Tomato-Basil Cream

4 (6 ounce) salmon fillets
salt and pepper
¼ cup olive oil
¼ cup white wine
1 cup chopped tomatoes
1 tablespoon fine chopped garlic
2 tablespoons chopped fresh basil
3 cups heavy whipping cream
2 tablespoons butter

Season salmon fillets liberally with salt and pepper.
Heat olive oil until very hot in a large sauté pan. Carefully
place salmon in pan. Cook until golden brown, approximately 4
minutes. Carefully turn salmon over. Add white wine and
reduce liquid until almost dry. Add tomatoes, garlic and basil.
Add whipping cream. Over medium temperature, reduce
cream until slightly thick. Add butter and adjust seasoning to
taste. **Serves 4**

Tracey Holmes

Magnolia Steak, Norfolk

A self-taught chef without a formal culinary education under her toque, Tracey Holmes has brought her natural talent to Ghent in Norfolk with Magnolia Steak. Chef Holmes and her husband David had lived in Ghent for ten years, so they knew where the culinary voids were. "We were remodeling our house and didn't have a kitchen, so we had to eat out for six months." That experience made Chef Holmes realize what type of restaurant the community needed. "We wanted to do something no one else was doing. We didn't want to copy another restaurant in the neighborhood. We wanted to add something to the locality."

Tracey's husband had experience in the retail business and had learned that it takes as much work to run a small business as it did a large one. So, he set out to locate a large restaurant site to house Tracey's dream. Meanwhile, Tracey traveled to Santa Fe and Dallas to research regional cuisine. Together they opened Magnolia Down South Cafe at the former Alexander's in Ghent. After initially experiencing moderate success, a name change and menu modifications turned the restaurant into a great success. "People thought we were a Mexican restaurant, and we weren't. It's Southwestern. Some people don't understand the difference. We changed a few items on the menu, added more beef, and changed the

name to Magnolia Steak. I don't know why, but it worked."

Chef Holmes serves a great deal of beef and salads at her restaurant. Her menu is varied, allowing anyone to find a dish they like. Though Magnolia Steak features the rich seasonings of the South West, its menu also offers milder entrees to appeal to those with less adventurous taste buds or those with dietary restrictions.

"I was born with a culinary passion. I adore it. My parents were social, so they weren't home a lot for dinner. It taught my brother Jimmy and I to cook for ourselves. My brother is a wonderful cook." With her professional start at Milton Warren's Icehouse Cafe in Virginia Beach, Chef Holmes waited tables and ventured into the kitchen as often as possible. "I also learned a great deal about food at The Captain's Table. I had access to the kitchen and all the equipment. That was fun and very educational. You learn a great deal working with other chefs. Now everything I do and everywhere I go is about food. I wake up in the middle of the night and write ideas down. It's my life!"

Chef Holmes' wish for her customers is that they truly enjoy themselves while at her restaurant. "Take your time. If people can come in, savor everything and slow down, I think they will enjoy themselves immensely.

I love to see groups of people ordering different items and tasting different dishes. Hit every category, even dessert. If you don't have room for dessert, just sit and relax – the room will come!"

Beyond the importance of good equipment, Chef Holmes' advice for the home cook is simple: "Finish what you start before you go on to something else. If you don't, you'll end up creating a huge mess in the kitchen, and have nothing to show for it. Fresh ingredients are important, but quality is the most important aspect. If you have good quality, human error is less of a factor."

Chef Holmes changes her menu approximately four times a year. Magnolia Steak has a large outdoor dining area, a beautiful indoor dining room, a bar and a billiards room. "We aren't just a restaurant. We're a total dining experience."

Guinness Beef and Cheese Grits Soufflé
with Guinness Mixed Mushroom Sauce

4 (8 ounce) center cut beef fillets

1 tablespoon olive oil

2 tablespoons unsalted butter

2 cloves garlic, finely chopped

½ teaspoon fresh ground black pepper

¼ teaspoon kosher salt

Cheese Grits Souffle (recipe to follow)

Guinness Mixed Mushroom Sauce

   (recipe to follow)

Combine butter, oil and seasoning to make a paste. Spread on both sides of steaks. Grill, broil or pan sauté until desired degree of doneness is achieved.

To assemble each, place ½ cup of Cheese Grits Soufflé in center of plate. Top with cooked fillet and cover with Guinness Mixed Mushroom Sauce. Serve with freshly blanched asparagus. **Serves 4**

Cheese Grits Soufflé

4 cups chicken stock

1 cup quick cooking grits

2 ounces unsalted butter

1 cup grated cheddar cheese

8 ounces cream cheese

2 tablespoons chopped pickled jalapeños

2 tablespoons Worcestershire Sauce

1 tablespoon Tabasco Sauce

3 eggs, well beaten

Preheat oven to 325°.

In a saucepan, bring chicken stock to a boil. Slowly add grits, whisking as you add. Reduce temperature and simmer approximately 5 minutes.

Stir in butter, cheeses, jalapeños, Worcestershire and Tabasco. Mix well. Incorporate eggs.

Place in a well greased casserole. Bake for 45-60 minutes or until well set. **Serves 4**

Guinness Mixed Mushroom Sauce

2 ounces unsalted butter

2 cups sliced mixed mushrooms

4 slices sugar cured bacon, diced

1 cup Guinness Stout

1 tablespoon diced parsley

1 tablespoon diced scallion

1 tablespoon diced cilantro

1 tablespoon diced chives

2 cups beef stock

¼ cup heavy cream

fresh ground black pepper

In a saucepan, melt butter over medium temperature. Add bacon and mushrooms. Sauté until bacon has rendered its fat. Add the Guinness Stout and herbs and reduce liquid by ¾. When this is complete, add beef stock and reduce until you have about 1½ cups of liquid. Add heavy cream and simmer for about 10 minutes. Add freshly ground pepper and adjust seasoning. **Serves 4**

Composed Salad

4 cups mixed salad greens

½ pound Gorgonzola cheese

2 cooked beets, diced

4 slices sweet red onion

½ cup toasted walnuts

Rice Wine Vinaigrette (recipe to follow)

Place salad greens on individual serving plates and top with cheese, beets, onions and walnuts. Drizzle with Rice Wine Vinaigrette.

Chef's Note: Composed Salad with Rice Wine Vinaigrette makes a nice last course for Guinness Beef meal.

Rice Wine Vinaigrette

1 cup rice wine vinegar

¾ cup olive oil

¼ cup Major Grey Chutney

½ teaspoon ground ginger

¼ cup chopped shallots

¼ cup fresh chopped parsley

¼ teaspoon kosher salt

fresh ground pepper

Combine all ingredients and mix well. Shake or stir before drizzling on salad.

Bobby Huber

Bobbywood, Norfolk

Following in the great footsteps of his father and grandfather, Chef Huber's love for cooking demonstrated itself at a very early age. Schooled in the Navy and at Johnson & Wales University, Norfolk, Chef Huber is strongly influenced by his travels to France, Italy, Norway, Germany, Canada and the U.S. Virgin Islands.

In keeping with his desire to never speak louder than necessary, Chef Huber doesn't scream to get his message across. This is apparent to the customers at Bobbywood as the staff dons headsets to quietly communicate to each other in their open kitchen.

"Working together as a team is essential in making a good restaurant a great restaurant. Also, if you constantly challenge your staff, they'll never get bored, and your customers will always benefit." Having a good time in the kitchen is essential for Chef Huber, and he is sometimes chided for joking around too much. "I've tried to change, but hey, life has to be fun." The food, however, is no joke. Chef Huber uses only the freshest ingredients available, changing his menu weekly to make use of seasonal products.

Starting his professional career at the early age of 12, Chef Huber washed dishes at Red Lobster. At 16, he worked at The Mango Tree in Cocoa Beach, Florida. "That was my first experience working in a gourmet restaurant." From there it was into the Navy for four years, where Chef Huber worked proudly for the submarine service. After deciding to stay in Norfolk, his career path took him down an exciting road from Caruso's Cellar to The Blue Crab, Sweet Bird of Youth, Fire and Ice, The Ship's Cabin, and finally to Bobbywood.

Born in New York and raised in Florida, Chef Huber currently resides in Hampton. Honorable and consumed with his profession, he lives to work and doesn't see himself doing anything else. "The restaurant business is my life." Being the chef and owner of a restaurant is more than a full-time job, it is a life calling.

Chef Huber's admiration for chefs with a Hollywood flair makes it easy to see how he came up with the name of his restaurant. His idols cook with a dramatic touch and are consummate showmen. "It's all part of the dining experience. Life is a stage for entertainers."

While Chef Huber enjoys foods that lean towards the comfort side, the menu at Bobbywood is eclectic, with staples including beef, chicken, seafood, and fresh vegetables.

His cooking philosophy is very simple: use fresh ingredients and never over-season or over-sauce foods. "Let the natural flavor come through."

Everyone at Bobbywood promises to make your evening a pleasant experience. "We want you to leave knowing that you got something special and that we care!"

Onion-Crusted Salmon Fillets with Spinach Potato Cakes and Sage Cream

To assemble each, place an Onion-Crusted Salmon Fillet over a Spinach Potato Cake and top with Sage Cream (all recipes follow). **Serves 4**

Onion-Crusted Salmon

4 (8 ounce) fresh salmon fillets, pin bones removed

salt and pepper to taste

1 onion, sliced in very thin circles

3/4 cup all-purpose flour

oil for frying

1 egg

4 tablespoons water

Season fillets with salt and pepper and set aside.

Toss the onions with 1/4 cup of the flour. In a skillet, heat oil and fry prepared onions until crispy. Place on a towel to drain. Place fried onions and remaining flour in a food processor and pulse until mixture resembles coarse cornmeal.

Preheat oven to 400°.

In a bowl, beat the egg with water to make an egg wash. Dip the flesh side of the salmon into the egg wash and then into the onion mixture, repeating until all salmon fillets are coated. Place on a greased cookie sheet and bake 15-20 minutes.

Spinach Potato Cakes

8 large Yukon gold potatoes , peeled and quartered

8 ounces spinach, washed, stemmed

2 eggs

2 ounces butter

1/4 cup milk

1 teaspoon salt

1/8 teaspoon white pepper

1/2 cup unseasoned bread crumbs

oil for sautéing

In a pot add potatoes and cover with water. Boil until soft and drain.

Place all ingredients for potato cakes except oil into a bowl and beat until very well mixed. Let mixture cool to touch, and form into cakes. Chill thoroughly.

Heat oil in a frying pan and sauté the cakes until brown on both sides. Place on a towel or cloth napkin to drain. Keep warm.

Sage Cream

1 cup heavy cream

1/2 cup chicken stock

2 sprigs fresh sage

pinch each of white, red, and black pepper

pinch of mace or nutmeg

Place all ingredients into a saucepan and bring to a boil. Reduce to a simmer and cook for approximately 15 minutes or until mixture coats the back of a spoon.

Oyster Stew

1 tablespoon unsalted butter

1 teaspoon chopped shallots

1 cup fresh corn kernels

1/8 teaspoon Tabasco Sauce

8 strips hickory-smoked bacon,
*   chopped and cooked crisp*

1 cup chicken stock

2 cups heavy cream

1 tablespoon fresh chives or chopped
*   green onions*

24 large oysters, shucked and liquor reserved

In a small saucepan, combine butter, shallots, corn, Tabasco and bacon. Cook on high heat until corn starts to "pop". Add stock and let reduce by half.

Lower temperature to medium and add cream and chives. Let mixture come to a boil and continue for 1 minute. Add oysters and reserved liquor. Bring back to a boil. Serve immediately. **Serves 4**

Chef's Note: At Bobbywood, the oyster stew is served over mashed potatoes!

Chocolate Amaretto Sin Pie

Oreo Cookie Crust

2 ounces butter, melted

32 Oreo Cookies

Pulverize the Oreos in a food processor until finely ground. Add melted butter and pulse to mix thoroughly. Press mixture along sides and into the bottom of a 9-inch springform pan. Chill crust for 5 minutes.

Chocolate Amaretto Filling

4 ounces butter

1 pound bittersweet chocolate

2 1/2 cups heavy cream

1 1/2 ounces Amaretto

To make filling, place butter and chocolate in the top of a double boiler and heat until melted. While constantly stirring, add half of the heavy cream, then the Amaretto, and then the rest of the heavy cream, mixing thoroughly, and remove from the double boiler. **(CAUTION:** *Remove double boiler from stove before adding Amaretto.***)**

Pour filling into the crust and let chill overnight. Unmold by running a warm towel over the sides of the springform pan. **Serves 12-16**

Spinach, Romaine and Arugula Salad Tossed with Garlic Dressing, Dried Tomatoes, Herb Croutons, Pecans, Gorgonzola Cheese and Grated Asiago Cheese

1 head romaine lettuce, picked and washed

10 ounces fresh spinach, stemmed and washed

8 ounces fresh arugula, picked and washed

$1/2$ cup chopped pecans

8 ounces crumbled Gorgonzola cheese

Garnish: grated Asiago cheese

Hand tear each of the greens. Refrigerate until ready to use.

Toss the salad mix with the dressing, pecans, Gorgonzola cheese, and dried tomatoes. Top with croutons and grated Asiago cheese. **Serves 4**

Garlic Dressing

6 anchovies

3 cloves garlic

$1/8$ teaspoon fresh ground black pepper

2 eggs

2 tablespoons Dijon Mustard

$1/4$ cup red wine vinegar

$1/4$ cup extra virgin olive oil

$1/4$ cup grated Parmesan cheese

Purée anchovies, garlic, pepper and eggs in a food processor. While the machine is running, add mustard and vinegar. Keep machine running and in a very thin yet constant stream, add the olive oil. Add Parmesan and incorporate well.

Dried Tomatoes

10 Italian plum tomatoes, quartered

1 tablespoon olive oil

1 teaspoon red wine vinegar

1 teaspoon salt

Preheat oven to 300°.

Mix together oil, vinegar and salt. Toss tomatoes into mixture. Lay tomatoes on a cookie sheet skin side down and bake in oven for 3 hours, turning the pan approximately every 30 minutes. Chill thoroughly.

Herb Croutons

$1/2$ loaf day old French bread cut into cubes

4 ounces melted butter

$1/4$ teaspoon onion powder

$1/4$ teaspoon thyme

$1/4$ teaspoon garlic salt

$1/4$ teaspoon dill

$1/4$ teaspoon ground oregano

$1/4$ teaspoon tarragon

$1/4$ teaspoon chopped basil

Preheat oven to 300°.

Mix all ingredients together thoroughly except bread cubes. Add bread cubes and toss. Bake on a cookie sheet in oven for 15-20 minutes or until golden brown.

Whole Roasted Pork Tenderloin with Fresh Cranberries and Spiced Rum-Vanilla Bean Reduction on Mashed Sweet Potatoes

Pork Tenderloin

2 cups water

½ cup granulated sugar

1 vanilla bean

1¼ cups Captain Morgan's Spiced Rum

2 pound pork tenderloin

salt and pepper to taste

oil for sautéing

10 ounces butter

1 cup fresh cranberries

Heat water in a saucepan until hot. Add the sugar and stir until dissolved. Add the vanilla bean and rum. Cover and let steep a minimum of 15 minutes.

Trim fat and silver skin from pork. Season with salt and pepper. Over medium temperature, heat enough oil to cover the bottom of the pan. Sear all sides of the pork (about 5 minutes per side). Drain off excess grease and add butter, cranberries and rum-vanilla sauce to the pan and bring to a boil. Lower heat to a simmer, and reduce sauce for 10 minutes.

Slice pork and arrange around Mashed Sweet Potatoes (recipe to follow) and pour sauce over the top. **Serves 4**

Chef's Note: The cooking time of the pork will vary depending on its thickness. If you prefer your pork cooked well to well done, place into a 350° oven after pan searing and let cook until desired degree of doneness is achieved.

Mashed Sweet Potatoes

4 large sweet potatoes, peeled and quartered

pinch of salt

10 ounces butter

2 tablespoons honey

¼ cup milk

pinch each of nutmeg, cinnamon, and allspice

Preheat oven to 350°.

Place potatoes in a pot and cover with water. Add salt and boil until soft.

Drain sweet potatoes and place on a cookie sheet. Bake in oven for 15 minutes. Remove from oven and place directly into a mixing bowl. Add butter and spices. Blend until smooth. Add honey and milk slowly and blend well.

Alain Jacqmin and Alvin Williams

Le Chambord/The Bistro, VA Beach

It's a global phenomenon at Le Chambord restaurant and its alter ego The Bistro in Virginia Beach, where proprietors Frank and Louisa Spapen searched as far abroad as Europe for Executive Chef Alain Jacqmin. Alain and his wife, Martine, came to the United States to cook Belgian cuisine for Le Chambord. Martine, whose previous expertise was in the beauty and fashion field, mastered the art of cold food presentation as *garde manger* in her family's catering business. Chef Jacqmin worked for Marcel Kreusch for over 20 years in his *Michelin Star* restaurants and attended culinary school in Europe for five years.

Before settling in the United States, Alain and Martine traveled through Europe to experience dining at world-class restaurants and resorts that boasted executive chefs with renowned reputations. "As a chef, I feel you are always learning something. It is very important to work with people who are interested in what they are doing. Before I am done in this business, I want to know how to cook everything."

Chef Alvin Williams hails from Leeds, England and is the Executive Chef at The Bistro. On a visit to the East Coast, Alvin decided he liked it so much that he wanted to stay. Before coming to the U.S., Chef Williams

attended the Thomas Danby Catering College for three years and fulfilled his apprenticeship at The Grovesnor House Hotel, Parklane. Chef Williams continued to work at the hotel for three more years. "I have worked for *Michelin Star* restaurants and learned many skills from great European chefs." In the United States, Chef Williams submitted his resume to many restaurants, but he really wanted to work with Alain at Le Chambord. "I took less money to work with Alain, but I have never regretted it. He can take a piece of fruit and prepare it in 50 different ways. Alain is a master."

Chef Alvin Williams' passion for cooking started when he was in diapers. "I remember always cooking for myself and my family. I like my kitchen to run smoothly. You've got to perfect the standards, and you always have to follow current food trends. If you continually show your staff new things, it helps in maintaining a healthy attitude in your kitchen. If they're interested, it also keeps me interested. An easy way to accomplish this is with seasonal menu changes."

Le Chambord and The Bistro run like clockwork due to the intelligence of these perfectionist chefs. Both agree that *mise-en-place* (everything in it's place) is the key to survival. "You must be organized and plan ahead. If you are ready, you can cook for one or one hundred people – you can handle whatever

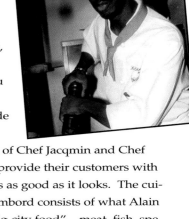

comes your way." Good equipment is also important, but these two chefs want you to know this does *not* include a microwave!

The goal of Chef Jacqmin and Chef Williams is to provide their customers with food that tastes as good as it looks. The cuisine at Le Chambord consists of what Alain likes to call "big-city food" — meat, fish, speciality appetizers and grand desserts. "It is food for the adventurous. I like to think of Le Chambord as a very special restaurant because the food and the ambience are a total package that will create a very enjoyable evening for anyone, whether you are a regular customer, or it is a special occasion."

At The Bistro, Chef Williams serves up large portions of hot food accompanied by good service. "We serve French-based foods with a modern accent. Our menu has an appealing presentation of comfort foods, and our atmosphere is more casual than Le Chambord."

Choose either restaurant for an enjoyable evening hosted by Frank and Louisa Spapen and savor a meal cooked by two European culinary maestros. The hardest part is deciding!

English Sherry Trifle

Layer One: Fruit Gelatin

½ bottle sherry

6 sheets of gelatin or 1½ (¼ ounce) envelopes

1 dash crème de cassis

¼ cup sugar

2 cups mixed seasonal fruit

6 ounces pound cake

     In a saucepan, reduce sherry by ⅓. (**CAUTION:** *Remove saucepan from stove before sherry.*) Add gelatin, crème de cassis and sugar. (**CAUTION:** *Remove saucepan from stove before adding creme de cassis.*) Stir until sugar is dissolved. Let cool slightly before pouring into a glass presention bowl or in individual wine glasses. Add fruit and top with pound cake. Place in refrigerator to set for at least 2 hours.

Layer Two: English Custard

2 cups milk

¼ cup flour

¾ cup sugar

1 tablespoon butter

4 eggs

2 dashes vanilla extract

pinch of nutmeg

     In a saucepan, bring milk to a boil. Remove from stove. In a bowl, whisk remaining ingredients together. Temper boiled milk into the bowl. Return mixture back to the saucepan. Return the saucepan to the stove and bring mixture back to a boil, stirring constantly. Remove from heat and let cool. Pour custard over the first layer in the glass bowl and refrigerate for 1 more hour.

Layer Three: Whipping Cream

2 cups heavy whipping cream

     Whip cream until stiff peaks form. Immediately before serving, place over the custard layer and garnish with fresh fruit. **Serves 12**

Chef's Note: English Sherry Trifle is a traditional English three layer dessert. For best presentation serve this dessert in a large, elegant glass bowl presented at the table or in individual wine glasses.

Chocolate Soufflé

4.5 ounces semisweet chocolate squares

4 tablespoons pastry cream (recipe to follow)

1 tablespoon + 1 teaspoon cocoa powder

2 tablespoons cognac

2 egg yolks

butter

3 tablespoons granulated sugar

6 egg whites

1/2 cup confectioners' sugar

Garnish: confectioners' sugar

Prepare pastry cream and set aside.

Preheat oven to 500°.

In a saucepan, carefully melt chocolate over low temperature. Fold in pastry cream, all cocoa powder, cognac and egg yolks.

Grease 4 (4-inch) soufflé bowls with butter. Coat butter with granulated sugar.

Whip egg whites until medium peaks form. Add confectioners' sugar and whip again. Fold egg white mixture into chocolate mixture. When fully incorporated, place mixture into prepared souffle bowls up to the lip. Bake in oven for 12 minutes. Dust with confectioners' sugar and serve warm. **Serves 4**

Pastry Cream

4 cups milk

1 vanilla bean

8 egg yolks

1 cup sugar

1/8 cup cornstarch

1/8 cup flour

Place milk and vanilla bean in a saucepan and bring to a boil. Turn off heat.

In a bowl, whisk egg yolks and sugar together until thick and light in color. Whisk in cornstarch and flour, incorporating completely. Slowly add heated milk while constantly whisking. Return mixture to the saucepan. Bring back to a boil and then simmer, continuing to whisk for 5 minutes.

Pour into a bowl or container. Place wax paper on top of the custard so a skin does not form and refrigerate until set.

Salmon Dijon with Herb Crust

4 (7 ounce) salmon fillets

salt and white pepper

2 tablespoons Dijon mustard

Herb Crust Mix (recipe to follow)

butter

Preheat oven to 425°.

Lightly season fillets with salt and white pepper. Spread a thin layer of Dijon mustard on one side (presentation side) of salmon and top with the herb crust mixture about 1/4-inch high.

Bake on a buttered baking sheet in oven for approximately 10-12 minutes. **Serves 4**

Herb Crust Mix

10 egg whites

2 tablespoons chopped dill

1 tablespoon chopped basil

2 tablespoons chopped tarragon

1 tablespoon chopped parsley

1 1/2 cups white bread crumbs

Whip egg whites until light and fluffy. Add freshly chopped herbs. Continue to whip egg whites and herbs until stiff peaks form. Gently fold in bread crumbs.

Appetizer of Twin Cheese Grilled Portobello Mushrooms with Sun-Dried Tomatoes

8 portobello mushrooms, stemmed

Portobello Mushroom Marinade (recipe to follow)

¼ cup sun-dried tomatoes

½ pound goat cheese

½ pound fresh mozzarella cheese, sliced

Garnish: watercress

Preheat oven to 350°.

Bake mushrooms in oven for 10 minutes. While mushrooms are still warm from the oven, pour marinade over them and set aside for 2 hours.

Heat grill. Grill mushrooms for 2-3 minutes on each side, and then place them on a baking sheet. Slice sun-dried tomatoes and place on the mushroom cap. Crumble goat cheese over sun-dried tomatoes and top with mozzarella.

Place mushrooms under broiler until cheese just begins to melt and is lightly golden. Serve with fresh watercress.

Serves 4

Portobello Mushroom Marinade

1½ tablespoons minced garlic

⅓ cup minced red onion

1 cup Port wine

2 tablespoons Dijon mustard

2 teaspoons dry sweet basil

1½ cups olive oil

1 teaspoon kosher salt

½ cup balsamic vinegar

Combine all ingredients together and mix well.

Duck Breast with Peaches (Caneton Aux Peaches)

4 duck breasts

oil for sautéing

4 fresh ripe peaches, quartered

1 cup bigarade sauce*

1 teaspoon apricot brandy

2 ounces butter

salt and pepper

Preheat oven to 450°.

Sauté duck breast over high temperature, skin side down. When golden brown, finish in oven until desired degree of doneness is achieved.

Sauté peaches in butter until soft.

In a separate saucepan, heat bigarade sauce until warm and add apricot brandy. (**CAUTION**: Remove saucepan from stove before adding brandy.)

To serve, slice duck breasts at an angle. Arrange duck around plate. Place peaches in center and spoon bigarade sauce over the top.

*Chef's Note: Bigarade sauce is a French brown sauce made basically of beef stock, duck drippings, orange and/or lemon juice. A good substitution for this sauce would be a demi-glace sauce enhanced with orange.

Seared Tuna with Rum Raisin Risotto

2 (8 ounce) tuna steaks or fillets

salt and pepper

2 plantains, thinly sliced

4 ounces butter

1 lemon

Rum Raisin Risotto (recipe to follow)

Lightly season tuna with salt and pepper. Pan-sear tuna and plantains in butter and a squeeze of lemon approximately 5 minutes per side or until desired degree of doneness is achieved. Serve with Rum Raisin Risotto. **Serves 2**

Rum Raisin Risotto

¼ cup dark rum

1½ cups soda water

1 cup raisins

½ pound orzo pasta

¼ pound mascarpone cheese

Combine rum and soda water. Soak raisins in mixture for 1 hour. Place orzo pasta in boiling salted water, stirring occasionally and cook until al dente. Drain pasta thoroughly. Add pasta to mascarpone cheese and mix thoroughly using a spatula. Strain raisins and add to the mixture. Mix thoroughly and keep warm.

Gazpaccio Espagnole

3 green peppers, diced

3 seedless cucumbers, diced

2 large tomatoes, diced

2 cups bloody mary mix

1 teaspoon fresh minced garlic

¼ cup olive oil

5 slices of bread, crust removed

¼ cup rice wine vinegar

salt and pepper

1 cup diced canned tomatoes and juice

2 teaspoons tomato purée

8 cups water

Garnish: fresh diced tomato concassé, chopped bell peppers, garlic croutons, fine diced onions and fine diced cucumbers

In a large bowl mix all ingredients together. Pour into a large food processor or blender and purée until smooth. Chill for 12 hours. Garnish and serve in chilled soup bowls. **Serves 12**

Sea Bass Chambord

4 (8 ounce) sea bass fillets

salt and pepper

2 cups white wine for poaching

2 stalks celery, fine dice

2 leeks, fine dice

3 tablespoons butter

1 cup White Wine Cream Sauce

   (recipe to follow)

1 teaspoon Dijon mustard

Garnish: chopped parsley

Prepare White Wine Cream Sauce and set aside.

Season fillets with salt and pepper. Poach fillets in white wine until fish is opaque and juices are milky white.

Braise celery and leeks in butter.

Warm the White Wine Cream Sauce and stir in Dijon mustard.

To assemble each, place a fillet in the center of a large preheated plate. Coat with sauce. Place braised vegetables over top of fillet and sprinkle with chopped parsley. **Serves 4**

White Wine Cream Sauce

1 cup fish stock

¼ bottle (750 ml) white wine

3 cups heavy whipping cream

1 tablespoon butter

In a saucepan over medium-high temperature reduce fish stock by half. Add wine and reduce by half. Reduce temperature to medium. Add whipping cream, stirring to incorporate. Add butter and stir.

Todd Jurich

Todd Jurich's Bistro, Norfolk

A self-made chef from the Pittsburgh area, Todd Jurich began cooking in the Tidewater area 20 years ago. He has attended culinary schools in both Switzerland and Thailand. Chef Jurich comes from a family of spectacular cooks. Using the freshest regional ingredients grown at his wife Barbara's organic garden on the Eastern Shore, Todd Jurich's Bistro features naturally raised products. Barbara also manages the front of the house at the Bistro, while Todd's sister, Kim, does the baking. Even his mother is in on the show, adorning the walls with her paintings and original artwork.

Chef Jurich's eclectic personality is discernable on the menu and on his expertly fashioned plates. "I'd title my cooking as American with nuances of Thai, Indian, Creole and French." As a chef, Todd feels it is very important to remain professional while staying relaxed. It is also of utmost importance to keep the lines of communication open. "A chef used to be a person that went around with blinders on. Now chefs have to look at the whole picture: how everything comes together to create a good experience for every customer. It's all a reflection on your food." Throughout his career, Chef Jurich has been a hands-on chef, and now he enjoys the privilege of stepping aside and delegating duties to his staff. "There is so much more than cooking for a chef to do, and those things are vital to a successful business. I really enjoy creating new dishes and designing new menus for the restaurant and special occasions."

Todd's discriminating palate has taught him to respect not only gourmets who render classic creations, but also those who have broken the mold with a light and contemporary approach to cooking. "Simplicity is the key to everything, especially food. If you use ingredients that you are familiar with and don't try to get too fancy, cooking should be an easy job and something you look forward to." Chef Jurich's immense knowledge of food can be seen in the masterpieces he constructs using simple core ingredients. "It's also very interesting to follow different foods through their courses in history and to watch how recipes have changed with the times."

Trying to edify his Tidewater customers with some European convictions, Chef Jurich endeavors to dissuade the public from eating just to live. He wants them to really enjoy dining. "Eating is a way of life in other countries. I think Europeans are one up on us in this category. We need to learn to respect food – to make mealtime a big part of our daily lifestyle."

The menu at the Bistro is constantly changing to reflect Chef Jurich's innovations and to take greatest advantage of the seasons.

Popular monthly wine dinners are coordinated with local representatives of wine makers, and usually consist of five courses and five to seven wines. These dinners are where Chef Jurich's true culinary genius glitters, taking charge of every tastebud throughout the entire meal, orchestrating a truly memorable evening. "It is really exciting creating an entire meal around wine. It is possibly the best way to present to the public your ideal combinations."

Success is a meager word when describing what Chef Jurich has achieved. The prosperity of the Bistro is due to a collection of proven techniques that keeps the customers coming back. "I think this is a very friendly place. You'll receive excellent service, eat excellent food, and enjoy unmatched quality at a good value."

Todd's Mom's Oyster Stew with Garlic Mashed Potatoes

Oyster Stew

3 cups heavy cream

$3/4$ teaspoon Worcestershire Sauce

pinch cayenne pepper

$1/4$ teaspoon white pepper

$1/2$ teaspoon cracked black pepper

$1/2$ cup chicken stock

$1/2$ teaspoon Old Bay Seasoning

2 dozen oysters, shucked, liquor reserved

$1 1/4$ cups lumpy Garlic Mashed Potatoes
(recipe to follow)

Garnish: $1/4$ pound bacon, fried crisp and diced, $1/2$ bunch fresh
chives, chopped and cracked black pepper

Scald heavy cream in a sauce pot over medium
temperature. Add Worcestershire, peppers, chicken stock, Old
Bay and oyster liquor and bring to a boil. Add oysters and
poach until edges curl, approximately three minutes.

To serve, place a dollop of Garlic Mashed Potatoes in a
soup bowl. Pour stew around potatoes. Garnish with bacon,
chives and cracked black pepper. **Serves 5**

Garlic Mashed Potatoes

2 tablespoons unsalted butter

6 large Idaho potatoes, peeled, large dice

2 heads garlic, roasted, peeled, mashed

2 teaspoons kosher salt

2 teaspoons cracked black pepper

$3/4$ cup hot half & half

Place potatoes in a large stock pot, cover with cold water
and bring to a boil. Add salt and reduce to a simmer. Cook
potatoes until just tender. Drain thoroughly and place back
into the pot. Add butter, garlic, salt and pepper. Pound with a
potato masher. Add half & half and mix thoroughly. Adjust
seasoning, butter and cream to taste and consistency.
Serves 5

Bittersweet Chocolate Torte with Double Vanilla Bean Sauce

Bittersweet Chocolate Torte

1 pound bittersweet chocolate chips,
   coarsely chopped
8 ounces unsalted butter, cut into ½" cubes
6 large eggs
butter for coating pan
Double Vanilla Bean Sauce (recipe to follow)

Preheat oven to 425°.

Line the bottom of an 8-inch springform pan with parchment paper. Butter the inside and bottom of pan. Wrap the outside of the pan with a double layer of heavy-duty foil to prevent seepage.

In a large metal bowl, combine the chocolate and butter. Set the bowl over a pan of hot water, stirring occasionally until chocolate is melted and smooth.

Crack eggs into a mixing bowl. Set mixing bowl over a pan of simmering water, and whisk the eggs constantly until they are warm to the touch. Remove from heat and beat with a mixer on high speed until soft peaks form and mixture has tripled in volume. Immediately pour half of the eggs into the chocolate mixture, blending well. Fold in the remaining eggs until well blended.

Pour into prepared pan. Set the prepared pan into a water bath. Bake for 5 minutes. Cover loosely with foil and bake for an additional 10 minutes.

Remove torte from water bath. Allow the torte to cool on a rack for 1 hour. Cover with plastic wrap and refrigerate for at least 3 hours before removing from the springform pan.

To unmold, run a knife around the sides of the torte and release the sides of the springform pan. Place a serving dish on top and invert. Remove the bottom of the pan and the parchment paper. Serve accompanied with Double Vanilla Bean Sauce. **Serves 12**

Double Vanilla Bean Sauce

4 cups heavy cream
1 vanilla bean
½ cup confectioners' sugar

Slice open vanilla bean lengthwise and scrape out the seeds. Place the bean into a sauce pot and add remaining ingredients. Bring to a boil and then reduce to a simmer. Cook 20 minutes, stirring occasionally. Refrigerate.

David Lapinski

The Omni Waterside Hotel, Norfolk

Which came first, the need to eat or the ability to cook? According to Chef David Lapinski, his appetite for superior dining could only be satisfied by becoming the accomplished chef he is today. "It's very rewarding to be able to cook and to satisfy your culinary desires." David is responsible for all food service at The Omni Waterside Hotel in Norfolk, including the 180-seat full-service restaurant, Riverwalk Cafe, Alexander's Bar, featuring bistro fare and nightly jazz, a kosher kitchen and the hotel's room service. He also handles special occasions such as banquets and holiday buffets. "It sounds like a lot, but if you stay organized, the number of guests you serve should never be a negative factor."

Chef Lapinski's career began almost 20 years ago as a line cook at Mount Holyoke College in Massachusetts. From there he took a position at Commander's Palace in New Orleans, and then worked both in New York and on the West Coast. He ventured to Tidewater in 1990 to work at the Cavalier Golf and Yacht Club in Virginia Beach, and finally to the Omni in 1993.

David's menu specialties highlight seafood, grilled meats and poultry. It is very challenging to create a menu that will please all of the Omni guests and visitors. "We have

people staying here from all over the world. You might have a group from the Midwest, one from the West Coast, and even from the Far East. Not everything is going to please all of those people, so our menu is fairly standard, focusing on typical American and regional dishes. However, the specialty board is where we can present more interesting and creative fare."

When planning his culinary ventures, David stresses the importance of looking at the whole menu. "Everything concerning a meal or an occasion is very important: whom you're serving, how certain foods are going to be conveyed and served, colors, temperature, textures, atmosphere, etc."

Chef Lapinski admires both international and local chefs who use unique regional ingredients in their cooking and take the time to present their creations in an original way. Like most chefs, David is a firm believer in eating out as often as possible to stay constantly challenged and educated on new trends and the public's tastes. "I feel strongly that chefs should be given a food allowance for eating out . . . you should try to experience fine dining or food prepared by a distinguished chef at a restaurant that desires to genuinely please its customers. It will open up a whole new

culinary world for you."

Chef Lapinski is a major part of why the Omni is a successful paragon in the Tidewater community. Consumed by a passion for food, David has a drive to achieve success in his vocation, especially since his daily duties can sometimes include very special occasions. "I have to be on top of my job every day. I'll try my best to do everything I can to make a wedding reception memorable, or someone's dinner at the Riverwalk Cafe or Alexander's Bar a special evening. We have a great reputation at the Omni, and a wonderful location. With so much going for us, I'll do my best to make everyone happy."

Risotto of Roasted Winter Vegetables

Risotto Base

1 cup diced celery

1 cup diced carrots

1 cup diced onions

4 ounces butter

1 pound Arborio rice

8-10 cups chicken stock

¾ -1 cup grated Parmesan cheese

Sauté celery, carrots and onions in 2 ounces of butter for 3 minutes. Add rice and stir to coat the grains evenly. Pour in 1⅔ cup chicken stock and bring to a boil. Reduce heat and simmer covered for 25 minutes.

Stir in remaining butter, Parmesan cheese, and 6-8 cups of chicken stock to the base at intervals over medium temperature until a smooth and velvety texture is achieved and the rice retains a slight crunch. The consistency of the Risotto should be pourable but not runny.

Vegetable Base

¾ cup chopped blanched broccoli

¾ cup chopped blanched fennel

¾ cup sliced leeks

½ cup yellow pepper strips

½ cup red pepper strips

2 cups sliced assorted mushrooms

¼ cup dried tomatoes, julienne

⅛ cup olive oil

salt and pepper

⅛ cup minced fresh seasonal herbs

Sauté vegetables over high temperature in olive oil and season with salt and pepper to taste and any fresh herb mixture you prefer. Place rice on plate and top with crisp, colorful vegetables. **Serves 8-10**

Chef's Note: For a more robust dish, add sautéed seafood or chicken to the vegetable base.

Phyllo Pastry Pockets with Portobello Mushrooms and Balsamic Dressing

3 tablespoons sliced garlic

1 teaspoon vegetable oil

½ tablespoon olive oil

⅛ cup sun-dried tomatoes, julienne

1 cup artichoke hearts

2 tablespoons sliced black olives

salt and pepper

Italian herbs

garlic salt to taste

8 sheets Phyllo pastry dough

melted butter as needed

¾-1 pound grilled or sautéed Portobello mushroom caps
   (season with salt and pepper)

1 cup leeks, julienne, fried in hot oil until crisp

½ cup Balsamic Dressing (recipe to follow)

Preheat oven to 400°.

Sauté garlic in oil just until garlic starts to turn brown.

In a separate bowl, combine olive oil, sun-dried tomatoes, artichoke hearts, black olives and seasonings. Add sautéed garlic and mix well.

Place 2 sheets of dough one on top of the other. Fold in half lengthwise and brush liberally with melted butter. Place ½ cup portion of the filling at the bottom of the folded dough, and begin to fold as you would a flag (in triangular shapes). Tuck any overlapping pastry underneath pocket. Brush again with melted butter and place on baking sheet. Repeat these steps until all sheets have been used. Bake in oven for 15-20 minutes or until nicely browned.

To assemble each, cut pocket to create 2 smaller triangles. Place cut ends face down at the top of a serving plate. At the bottom the plate, place sliced Portobello mushrooms, fanned out. Sprinkle the fried leeks onto the center of the plate and drizzle Balsamic Dressing over the mushrooms. **Serves 4**

Chef's Note: Keep a slightly damp cloth over the pastry when not working with it to prevent it from drying out.

Balsamic Dressing

¼ cup Balsamic vinegar

2 tablespoons rice vinegar

½ cup whole grain mustard

pinch of salt

½ teaspoon pepper

½ teaspoon sugar

¾ cup olive oil

Combine all ingredients in a bowl except olive oil. While whipping, add the olive oil until well incorporated.

Shrimp and Crawfish Capellini

7 tablespoons vegetable oil

¾ cup all-purpose flour

¾ cup diced onion

¾ cup diced celery

⅓ cup diced green bell peppers

⅓ cup diced red bell peppers

1½ teaspoons Cajun seasoning

2 ounces butter

1 pound medium shrimp, peeled

3 cups shrimp stock or clam juice

⅛ cup Worcestershire Sauce

1 cup evaporated skim milk

1 cup heavy cream

2 teaspoons minced garlic

1 pound crawfish tail meat

3 pounds cooked Capellini pasta

    (about 1½ pounds raw weight)

Garnish: whole cooked crawfish, sliced scallions,
        and Cajun seasoning

    In a heavy skillet, heat oil over high temperature until it begins to smoke. With a whisk, gradually mix in the flour, stirring until smooth. Continue cooking, whisking constantly until roux is a dark red-brown. (Be careful not to let it scorch in the pan.) Remove from heat and immediately stir the next 5 ingredients with a wooden spoon. Continue stirring for another 5 minutes.

    In a 4-quart saucepan, melt the butter over medium-high temperature. Add the shrimp and sauté until they turn pink, stirring often. Add the roux to the pan and cook until smooth. Gradually add remaining ingredients except pasta, liquids first, stirring after each addition. Bring stew to a boil, simmer for 2 minutes and remove from heat. Adjust seasonings.

Serve stew over the pasta garnishing each with hot, whole crawfish, sliced scallions, and Cajun seasoning.
Serves 8

Gazpacho with Avocado and Bay Shrimp

3 cups tomato concassé, small dice

1 cup V-8 juice

1½ cups thinly sliced scallions

½ tablespoon minced garlic stirred into
    1½ cups cold water to disperse evenly

¼ cup diced red bell pepper

¼ cup diced yellow bell pepper

¼ cup diced green bell pepper

1 cup peeled, seeded, and diced cucumber

1 teaspoon salt

fresh ground black pepper to taste

1 beef bullion cube

1 tablespoon cider vinegar

1 tablespoon olive oil

2 tablespoons minced cilantro

1 ripe avocado, skinned, small dice

2 cups cooked small shrimp

Garnish: cilantro sprigs and sliced limes

    Combine all ingredients except avocado and shrimp in a large bowl. Gently stir in shrimp and avocado and incorporate well. Chill before serving.

    Garnish with cilantro and sliced lime. **Serves 6**

Bread Pudding Soufflé with Bourbon Sauce

Bread Pudding

2½ cups bread pudding (your favorite recipe)

4 egg yolks

¼ cup granulated sugar

6 egg whites

½ cup confectioners' sugar

Bourbon Sauce (recipe to follow)

Preheat oven to 350°.

Place bread pudding in a large mixing bowl and set aside.

In the top of a double boiler over very low temperature, whip egg yolks and granulated sugar with a wire whisk until frothy and shiny. Whip mixture into bread pudding until well blended and smooth.

In a mixing bowl, beat egg whites until frothy, using an electric mixer. Gradually add the confectioners' sugar and beat until egg whites form stiff peaks. Gently fold egg white mixture into the bread pudding mixture.

Butter and lightly flour a 1½-quart soufflé dish. Fold in bread pudding mixture. Bake in oven for 35-40 minutes. Serve immediately, topped with Bourbon Sauce. **Serves 8**

Bourbon Sauce

½ pound unsalted butter

½ pound brown sugar

¼ cup bourbon

½ cup heavy cream

Heat butter and brown sugar over medium-high temperature until melted and thoroughly combined. Add bourbon. (**CAUTION:** *Remove pan from stove before adding bourbon. If bourbon ignites when returned to the flame, stir until flame extinguishes.*) Turn off heat and stir in cream.

Meredith Nicolls
The Resort at Powhatan Plantation, Williamsburg

An Eastern Shore native born in Bayford, Virginia, Meredith Nicolls brings his regional Virginia cooking to The Resort at Powhatan Plantation. Following his own path through a variety of careers, Meredith's creativity finally led him in a culinary direction. His first apprenticeship was under the distinguished Dominique D'Ermo of Dominique's in Washington, D.C. Meredith has worked with Tidewater locals Marcel Desauliniers, Amy Brandt and Todd Jurich. In 1987 he opened his own restaurant, Meredith's, located inside Virginia Beach's exclusive furniture store, Willis Wayside. Four years later he started cooking at The Resort at Powhatan Plantation in Williamsburg.

Chef Nicolls has always been interested in cooking. Growing up in a family that entertained often, Meredith was surrounded by an exceptional culinary base. In addition, he was able to reap the benefits from the surrounding bounty of the Eastern Shore. "I grew up with these things, so I had a great deal of exposure at a young age. I think that sparked the interest I had for cooking into a passion."

Meredith has a very basic philosophy on how a kitchen should be run, and it begins with one key element: organization. "If you are unorganized, what you are trying to produce won't come out in a proper fashion. In addition, your demand for organization

becomes greater with the higher number of distractions you have to contend with."

The Resort at Powhatan Plantation is a time-share community that includes two restaurants, The Kitchen at Powhatan Plantation and The Powhatan Room. In the early evening, it's showtime for this performing artist. "I realized early that my staff and I have to be good every day, because we have a different audience every day and their expectations are always high. If we cook within our level of expertise . . . we will always succeed. If you come to our restaurants with the expectation of receiving a very good meal surrounded by a charming atmosphere and friendly service, then we can meet and perhaps exceed your expectations. If we do this consistently, then we'll accomplish what we should."

When deciding what to cook at your house, Meredith hopes that you consider all aspects of the venture before you start. Keep it simple, and most importantly – always use fresh ingredients. "You never want to over-complicate food." Stressing the importance of wine as a food companion, Meredith feels that beverage selection should be contemplated carefully. "The meal should be a marriage of food and wine. Wine was made and produced to go with food and can really play an important part in the success of a meal."

Utilizing a food at its natural peak is vital, and can make a good dish better. To gain a good culinary background, Chef Nicolls suggests adding variety to your daily diet which will in turn kindle creativity. "Relax, get the family together, give respect and thanks, engage in splendid conversation and enjoy your meal – really savor it."

The atmosphere at The Kitchen at Powhatan Plantation is 18th century colonial. It embodies charm, romance and simplicity. "All of the attributes here place more focus on the foods we serve. Our restaurant isn't a showplace or garbled with glittery effects. Our 200 year old china pattern, which is pure white, becomes the frame for the food served on it. We want you to look at the food, notice how beautiful it is, and let the zephyrs entice you. Then you'll want to eat, not look around!"

Pirate's Style Fish Stew

¼ *cup olive oil*

½ *cup diced celery*

½ *cup diced onion*

½ *cup diced fennel*

½ *cup diced carrot*

1 *cup tomato concassé with juice*

1 *clove garlic, minced*

salt and pepper

1 *bottle (750 ml) dry white wine*

½ *gallon Fish Fumet (recipe to follow)*

8 *small red bliss potatoes, small dice*

1 *cup peas or green beans*

1½ *teaspoons cayenne pepper*

2½ *pounds assorted fish fillets cut into*
   2 *ounce pieces*

1 *tablespoon fresh thyme*

1 *tablespoon fresh oregano*

1 *tablespoon finely chopped fresh parsley*

pinch of saffron

1 *teaspoon lemon juice*

corn bread

In a heavy bottomed stock pot, heat oil until hot. Add celery, onion, fennel and carrot and sweat (covered) until soft. Add tomato concassé with juice and cook 3-4 minutes. Add garlic. Season lightly with salt and pepper. Add wine and bring to a boil. Add Fish Fumet and return to a boil. Add potatoes, peas, and cayenne pepper and stir well.

Cook enhanced fumet until vegetables are al dente. Add fish fillets and cook 5 minutes. Add remaining herbs, lemon juice and salt and pepper to taste. Serve hot in large bowls with toasted corn bread. **Serves 8**

Fish Fumet

¼ *cup oil*

1½ *cups sliced onion or white part of leek*

1½ *cups sliced carrots*

1½ *cups sliced celery*

1½ *cups sliced fennel*

3-5 *pounds clean fresh white fish bones*
   (*no gills, guts or scales*)

4 *bay leaves*

zest of 2 lemons

4-6 *sprigs fresh parsley*

6-8 *whole black peppercorns, cracked*

½ *bottle (750 ml) dry white wine*

In a heavy bottomed stock pot, heat oil and add all vegetables. Sweat until just soft. Add fish bones, bay leaves, lemon zest, parsley, and peppercorns and continue to cook approximately 5 more minutes. Add white wine and bring to a boil. (**CAUTION**: *Remove pot from stove before adding wine.*) Add just enough cold water to cover bones. Return to a boil, skimming off any fat or foam. Reduce temperature and simmer for approximately 45 minutes. Continue skimming off any fat or foam as needed.

Strain through a fine sieve. Pass through fine cheese cloth 2 times. Place into several separate containers to cool. Refrigerate until use or freeze for future use. **Makes 1 gallon**

Citrus Cheese Pudding

2 pounds cream cheese

8 eggs

⅓ teaspoon pure vanilla extract

1½ cups refined or turbinado sugar

juice and zest of 1 lemon

juice and zest of 1 lime

juice and zest of 1 orange

8 ounces sour cream

Preheat oven to 300°.

In a food processor, purée the cream cheese, eggs, vanilla and sugar until smooth. Add citrus juices and zest and sour cream. Mix until incorporated.

Line the bottom of an 8-inch springform pan with heavy aluminum foil. Fill springform with the pudding mixture.

Bake in a water bath for approximately 1 hour. (The pudding should be well set, but not cracking.) Remove from oven and remove from water bath. Allow to cool. Refrigerate at least 6 hours before serving. **Serves 8**

Chef's Note: This pudding can also be cooked in individual ovenproof serving molds.

Pistachio-Breaded Flounder with Brown Butter

4 (7 ounce) flounder fillets

¼ cup flour

egg wash

1 cup pistachios, ground fine

1 tablespoon canola oil

3 tablespoons unsalted butter

splash of vermouth

splash of lemon juice

Preheat oven to 500°.

Coat fillets lightly with flour. Dip in egg wash and roll in ground pistachios. Set aside.

Over medium temperature, heat oil in a skillet. Add fillets and cook on both sides until pistachios are golden, being careful not to burn. Remove from skillet and place in an ovenproof dish. Finish cooking in oven for approximately 5 minutes.

Return skillet to stove over high temperature and add butter. Heat until the butter starts to brown slightly. Add a splash of vermouth and lemon juice. (*CAUTION: Remove skillet from stove before adding vermouth*). Pour over fish fillets while still hot. **Serves 4**

Chicken, Veal and Shiitake Mushroom Terrine

2 teaspoons canola oil

1 shallot, finely diced

1½ cups shiitake mushrooms, stems removed,
   fine julienne

2 pounds boneless, skinless chicken breasts

⅓ pound unsalted fatback

⅓ cup cream

1 egg

salt and pepper

1 pound lean trimmed veal, cut into small cubes

mix of cayenne pepper, paprika and black
   pepper to taste

1 pound caul fat*

2 bay leaves

1 large sprig rosemary

2 sprigs thyme

Preheat oven to 400°.

Heat oil to hot in a sauté pan. Sauté shallot and mushrooms until juices are released. Remove from heat and let cool.

In a food processor, purée chicken, fatback, cream and egg until smooth. Be careful not to overwork the mixture. Season with a pinch of salt and pepper. Place chicken mixture in a large bowl. Fold in mushrooms and shallots.

Season all sides of veal cubes with cayenne mix. Then fold veal cubes into chicken mixture.

Line a 1½-quart terrine mold with caul fat leaving enough excess to cover the top of the terrine. Carefully fill the mold. Use a spatula to pack corners and smooth top.

Cover the terrine with caul fat making sure to get a good seal. Place bay leaves, rosemary and thyme on top of terrine.

Bake 45 minutes or until just firm to touch. Remove from oven and allow to cool, approximately 30 minutes. Refrigerate overnight. Unmold to serve. **Serves 10**

Chef's Note: Caul fat can be purchased from your butcher.

Roast Muscovy Duck Breast

1 (1 pound) Muscovy duck breast

salt and pepper to taste

Preheat oven to 450°.

Split duck breast in half. Remove half of the fat from the duck breast, leaving the remaining half attached to the flesh. Salt and pepper the breast to taste. Place the breast in a very hot skillet, skin side down, cooking approximately 15-20 minutes. As fat is being rendered, baste the flesh a few times using a spoon. Be sure to baste all of the flesh and to get a good sear. Place the breast in oven for approximately 5-7 minutes, or until desired degree of doneness is achieved, basting 2 or 3 times more. Remove from oven. Allow to rest 5 minutes before slicing. **Serves 2**

Edward Nowakowski

The Norfolk Waterside Marriott, Norfolk

Trained in classical European cuisines, Chef Edward Nowakowski has elegantly adapted his cooking style for Tidewater customers – easily satisfying even the most adventuresome.

Chef Nowakowski was born in Linz, Austria, and raised in Poland. There he attended three years of restaurant school, including one year of Master Chef training. His apprenticeship was fulfilled in several European cities including Lyon, France, where Chef Nowakowski specialized in the art of *charcuterie* (the fancy presentation of cold meat). "Presentation is a very important part of taste. It is the vision of the food that establishes your appetite. Also, the taste of the food has to keep up with the visual creation."

Upon arriving in the United States in 1977, Chef Nowakowski started working at the Grand Hyatt Hotel in New York. Cooking in a large kitchen was completely different from his European training. "In a large kitchen you work with other chefs and you don't get to physically work on each dish because of time limitations. My favorite thing is to give each dish a special touch. You can't devote that much time to each dish personally. You have to trust someone else to do part of it."

Before coming to the Norfolk Marriott as Executive Chef, Edward worked at the Mandalay Four Seasons Hotel in Texas; the Registry Hotel in Minnesota; the Norfolk Airport Hilton and the Holiday Inn Hotel and Conference Center in Virginia. He now resides in Virginia Beach with his wife Maria. His son Robert also lives in Virginia Beach, and his daughter Julia lives in Poland.

Chef Nowakowski has received many awards for his *garde manger* work and his ice sculpting, including one gold medal, four bronze medals, and many other honors. "Ice carving was a new thing for me. We didn't do that in Europe. One day the Executive Chef where I worked asked who knew how to do an ice carving. I had never done one before, but I raised my hand to say that I knew how. The assignment was a horse. I went to the souvenir store and bought a miniature horse statue. I set it up with a light behind it to cast a shadow on the wall, and traced it and used it as my pattern to carve the ice horse. I've learned a lot about ice carving since then – enough to be the best in the area." Chef Nowakowski has also won awards for his tallow sculptures, including a first place in the "showpiece" category from the local chapter of the American Culinary Federation's food show for his rendition of King Neptune. Edward is also famous for his chocolate and coconut paintings.

Old traditions are hard to find in the modern kitchens of today. Chef Nowakowski feels shortcuts have hurt the culinary industry because the modern kitchen uses too many prefabricated products, even for the simplest things. "A good chef always has the four basic stocks in the refrigerator: fish, chicken, beef, and a demi-glace or brown sauce. This enables a chef to have a good basis for any dish he desires to make."

The success of the Norfolk Marriott starts in the kitchen. "From sanitation to service, everything has to harmonize together. Servers must be friendly and educated, and should be able to introduce you to new items."

Chef Nowakowski thinks that he has a great job. "I am very happy to be the chef, and I feel very fortunate. I try to learn something new every day. You have to constantly upgrade what you know to keep the next customer happy."

Chicken-Mango Casserole

1 (2 pound) chicken, quartered, back and neck bones removed

salt and pepper to taste

olive oil for frying

2 cups sliced mango

lemon juice to taste

1 tablespoon cornstarch

water

Garnish: orange, kiwi, and star fruit

Season chicken with salt and pepper. In heavy pan heat oil and fry chicken until light brown.

Meanwhile, force ripe mango through a sieve, or purée. Add lemon juice.

Pour mango mixture over chicken. Simmer until chicken is done.

Mix 1 tablespoon of cornstarch with cold water to form a pourable thick liquid and stir into the casserole a little at a time until desired consistency is obtained. Bring to boiling point. Do not overcook. Garnish with orange, kiwi, and star fruit slices. **Serves 4**

Marinated Salmon for the Grill

1½ pound salmon fillet

¾ cup sugar

¼ cup salt

3 tablespoons crushed white peppercorn

3 tablespoons fresh dill

oil

Wipe salmon with a cloth and dry well. Rub all sides of salmon with sugar, salt, crushed white peppercorn and fresh dill.

Cut salmon into desired size portions. Place pieces one on top of the other. Cover with a weighted plate and marinate for 20-22 hours (2 hours at room temperature, and then 18-20 hours in the refrigerator).

Keeping as intact as possible, remove skin. Cut skin into 1 inch strips. Oil lightly and grill with salmon over charcoal. Serve the crisp skin with the salmon fillet. **Serves 3-4**

Chef's Note: Sweet and sour mustard sauce is a good addition to the meal.

Lobster Ragoût

1 tablespoon minced onion

1 cup sliced mushrooms

2 tablespoons butter

3 cups cubed lobster meat

1 teaspoon lobster base

1 tablespoon flour

pinch of dry mustard

salt and pepper to taste

4 cups heavy whipping cream

Sauté onion and mushrooms in butter for 5 minutes. Add lobster meat and lobster base and toss. Reduce heat and sprinkle with flour, dry mustard, salt and pepper. Toss again and cook for 5 minutes. Add cream and simmer, stirring constantly until liquid begins to thicken. Serve as a main dish on rice or as an appetizer in pastry shells. **Serves 6 as a Main Dish**

Frozen Raspberry Soufflé

½ cup raspberry juice

½ cup sugar

4 egg yolks

2 cups heavy cream, whipped

1 tablespoon raspberry liqueur

Garnish: fresh raspberries and ½ cup heavy cream, whipped

Boil raspberry juice and sugar to a syrup. Remove from stove and cool slightly. Add egg yolks, beating well with a wire whisk.

Add raspberry liqueur, blending gently. Fold in whipped cream. Pour into a soufflé dish or dessert glasses and freeze a minimum of 4 hours before serving. Garnish with fresh raspberries and whipped cream. **Serves 4**

Ricotta, Tomato and Scallion Spread on Rye Toast Points

14 ounces ricotta cheese

¼ cup cream

salt and pepper to taste

lemon juice to taste

1½ cups diced tomato

1 diced scallion

rye toast points

Garnish: tomato wedges, cucumber slices and fresh minced dill

Mash cheese with a fork. Add cream, salt, pepper and lemon juice. Fold in tomatoes and scallion. Spread mixture on rye toast points. Garnish with tomato wedges and cucumber slices. Sprinkle with fresh dill. **Serves 6**

Chef's Note: This also makes a great sandwich filling.

Bluefish Fillet Stuffed with Backfin Crabmeat and Served with Virginia Riesling and Green Spicy Butter Sauces

1¼ pounds crabmeat, picked over

¼ pound sea scallops

½ cup heavy cream

¼ teaspoon fresh lemon juice

salt and pepper

¼ cup chopped leeks

⅛ cup diced white mushrooms

3 tablespoons butter

4 (6 ounce) bluefish fillets

4 sheets puff pastry

Preheat oven to 375°.

Place crabmeat and scallops in blender and blend until smooth. Add cream, lemon juice, salt and pepper. Blend until smooth.

Sauté leeks and mushrooms in butter. Add to mousse and set aside.

For each serving, lay bluefish fillet on top of puff pastry and place a portion of mousse on top. Form a fish shape. Be creative! Bake in oven until golden brown, approximately 20 minutes. Serve with Virginia Riesling and Green Spicy Butter Sauces (Recipes to follow). **Serves 4**

Virginia Riesling Sauce

4 small shallots, minced

½ clove garlic, minced

1 tablespoon butter

½ cup Virginia Riesling wine

6 black peppercorns

2 cups heavy cream

salt and pepper

Cook shallots and garlic in butter over very low temperature in a covered pot until juices begin to release, but do not brown. Deglaze with wine. (**CAUTION**: *Remove pot from stove before adding wine.*) Add black peppercorns. Reduce by ¾. Add heavy cream and reduce until sauce coats the back of a spoon. Season with salt and pepper. Strain through fine cloth. Return to pan and gently reheat before serving.

Green Spicy Butter Sauce

8 cups fish stock

4 small shallots, chopped

⅓ cup chopped parsley

⅓ cup chopped fresh spinach

⅓ cup chopped fresh basil

4 ounces sweet butter, softened

salt and pepper

Bring fish stock to a boil and reduce by half. In a separate saucepan, sauté shallots, parsley, spinach and basil in 2 tablespoons of butter. Add to stock. Reduce again by half or until syrupy. Blend sauce (with a hand blender right in pan or in a standing blender) until smooth. Reheat and add small pieces of butter until desired consistency of sauce is obtained. Season with salt and pepper to taste. Serve warm, but not hot.

Rock Shrimp and Sweet Corn Ravioli with Cracked Black Pepper Sauce

1 ear of corn

¼ pound rock shrimp, peeled and deveined

½ cup heavy cream

salt and white pepper to taste

1 teaspoon fresh chopped chives

15 wonton wrappers

egg wash

1 shallot, diced fine

¼ bay leaf

pinch of thyme leaf

4 whole peppercorns

1 cup white wine

juice of 1 lemon

1 pound unsalted soft butter, cut in small pieces

Garnish: 5 freshwater prawns or large shrimp,
**   cracked black pepper, and corn**

Remove kernels from cob by running a paring knife through the center of the corn kernels (while on cob) from top to bottom all around the ear of corn. Then scrape the kernels from the cob with the back of a knife. Retain pulp and juice separately. Over low temperature, reduce the juice from the corn by half. Cool and add back to kernels.

In a food processor blend shrimp, heavy cream and half of the corn. Season with salt and white pepper. Add chives.

Lay out wonton wrappers and roll to half their original thickness. Brush with egg wash. Place 1 tablespoon of the shrimp mixture on one side of each wrapper. Fold, seal and vent wrapper. Poach in boiling salted water for 4 minutes.

Place remaining ingredients, except butter in a small saucepan. Bring to a boil, then simmer until reduced by half. Begin whisking in butter one piece at a time until it is all incorporated. Season with salt and white pepper. Strain sauce.

For garnish, poach fresh water prawns and remaining corn in simmering salted water for 3 minutes. Place hot ravioli on plate. Spoon sauce over each one and garnish with fresh water prawn, corn, and cracked black pepper. **Serves 3**

Susan Painter

Cafe Rosso, Norfolk

A vacation in New Orleans and a fascination with superior cuisine swayed Chef Susan Painter towards her culinary career. Most of her history is charted along the East Coast from Pennsylvania to Virginia at a variety of dining establishments, locally including Ship's Cabin, Bella Monte, and most recently, Cafe Rosso.

Running her kitchen professionally and proficiently, Susan always strives to keep an open mind and remain approachable to her staff. However, Susan knows exactly what she wants. "In my kitchen, I definitely like things done my way. I always hire people who are bright and have a good sense of humor. Experience is not of the utmost importance to me, but my employees have to show an interest in cooking. If someone shows promise or talent, I'll run with it."

Susan tries to steer clear of health taboos such as cream and salt, but she does admit to vises, olive oil and sugar. "I really like to cook using fresh produce, but I also have a realistic approach to cooking." While working at Bella Monte, Chef Painter had a lot of latitude in cooking Italian and Mediterranean fare, and she introduced new and exciting dishes to customers who craved more than the average pasta repast. "Some of my favorite dishes to cook are Pacific rim recipes, but they can take

a great deal of time. It is so rewarding to serve a customer that is looking for something exciting to eat. It allows a chef to get very creative." Much of Susan's inspiration comes from chefs that really understand food, knowing each ingredient for what it is and for what it can do. "In a world filled with an 'anything goes' rational, you have to know where to draw the line." At Cafe Rosso, Susan is once again working with owner Joe Hoggard. These two talented forces working together is a culinary victory for the Tidewater area.

Talented yet modest, Susan acknowledges that she works extremely hard. "This culinary passion is something – once you realize you have it, you have no choice but to act on it." Her pride shows on the plates she presents, and her hard work is recognized by her contented consumers. "There's also a difference between an ego and confidence. You have to work really hard at not getting a swelled head. Just take your accomplishments and use them to believe in yourself."

In the Tidewater area, Susan suggests that all cooks, both professional and domestic, take full advantage of harvests from local farmers and fishermen and by using indigenous meats, produce and seafood whenever possible. "Not only will your foods taste better because you will be using the freshest

ingredients available, but you'll be supporting the local economy as well." She advises that you will be a happier cook if you remain flexible and don't follow a recipe too strictly.

Recently returning from a vacation in Europe, Susan traveled through Italy savoring the beautiful countryside and the exceptional cuisine. "You can learn about food anywhere you are. The knowledge you gain from visiting a European country is second to none, and I plan on using this experience to enhance my cooking and menu planning at Cafe Rosso." Tidewater diners get ready! A trip to Europe for you is as close as 21st street in Ghent, with Chef Susan Painter as your culinary tour guide.

Sun-Dried Tomato and Applewood-Smoked Bacon Polenta with Sautéed Scallops

1 cup dried polenta (not instant)

1 quart chicken stock

2 ounces unsalted butter, cut into small pieces

6 sun-dried tomatoes in oil, chopped and drained

4 slices applewood-smoked bacon,
      cooked golden brown, fine dice

4 ounces grated Romano cheese

2 ounces melted butter

12 sea scallops

flour for dredging

Combine polenta and cold chicken stock and stir over medium temperature until boiling. Reduce temperature to low and continue cooking for about 1 hour, stirring occasionally. If polenta gets too thick, add a little more chicken stock or water. Add butter, tomatoes and bacon and stir until butter melts. Pour polenta into a buttered 9x12-inch pan and chill a minimum of 2 hours. (This can be prepared 2-3 days ahead.)

Preheat oven to 350°.

Remove polenta from refrigerator and cut into 12 squares or cut into various shapes with cookie cutters. Dredge each polenta piece in flour, shaking off excess. Brush with butter and roast for 15 minutes in oven.

Sauté lightly floured scallops until done and place one scallop on top of each piece of polenta. You can also top this with your favorite chutney. **Serves 12**

Orecchiette and Spinach Pasta

8 ounces pancetta, diced

2 tablespoons olive oil

1 cup sliced mushrooms

4 cloves garlic, minced

4 rounded tablespoons tomato paste

1 cup chicken stock

12 ounces dried orecchiette, cooked al dente

1 pound spinach, washed, stems removed

salt and pepper to taste

Sauté pancetta in olive oil until it turns golden brown. Add mushrooms and sauté 1-2 minutes. Add garlic and sauté briefly. Add tomato paste and chicken stock stirring to blend well. Bring mixture to a boil and reduce temperature. Add the pasta and spinach. Allow the spinach to cook briefly. Check seasonings and serve immediately. **Serves 4**

Chef's Note: This dish is excellent served with grilled chicken or sautéed shrimp.

Portobello Mushroom Pâté

2½ cups finely diced Portobello mushrooms

2 tablespoons butter

2 tablespoons olive oil

1 large shallot, minced

2 cloves garlic, minced

salt and pepper to taste

1 (6 ounce) boneless, skinless chicken breast, cubed

2 large eggs

¼ cup heavy cream

¼ cup grated fresh Romano cheese

⅓ pound pancetta, thinly sliced

Preheat oven to 325°.

Over medium temperature, sauté mushrooms in butter and olive oil. Add shallot and garlic. Season liberally with salt and pepper. Sauté mixture until the mushrooms give off their liquid and the liquid is cooked off. Set mixture aside and allow to cool.

In a food processor, combine mushroom mixture, chicken breast, eggs, cream and Romano cheese. Season again with salt and pepper. Process until well combined.

Pour mixture into a 10x3x3-inch pâté pan or a small loaf pan that has been lightly oiled and lined with the pancetta. Bake pâté in a water bath approximately 40-50 minutes or until the internal temperature reaches 170°. If pancetta browns too quickly, cover pâté with aluminum foil.

Remove from oven and chill thoroughly. Slice and serve with warm bruschetta or crackers.

Panzanella

stale, toasted Italian bread, large dice

5 tomatoes, cut in a large dice

1 yellow pepper, roasted and diced

1 red pepper, roasted and diced

8 cloves garlic, chopped

½ cup Italian parsley, chopped

½ cup basil, chopped

½ cup Alfonso olives, pitted and halved

½ stalk celery, diced

½ cup extra virgin olive oil

3 tablespoons red wine vinegar

salt and cayenne pepper to taste

Combine all ingredients except bread and tomatoes and allow to marinate 1-2 hours. Toss with bread and tomatoes. Adjust seasoning and serve.

Pine Nut-Crusted Rockfish with Arugula Pesto

¼ *cup pine nuts*

¾ *cup seasoned croutons*

Arugula Pesto (recipe to follow)

6 (6 ounce) rockfish fillets

oil

Preheat oven to 350°.

Combine pine nuts and croutons in food processor and process lightly. Top rockfish with arugula pesto, then roll in crouton-crumb mixture. Place on a lightly oiled baking sheet and bake 10-15 minutes. **Serves 6**

Arugula Pesto

1 cup extra virgin olive oil

¼ *cup Romano cheese*

6 garlic cloves

4 cups Arugula

⅓ *cup toasted pine nuts*

salt and pepper to taste

Process all ingredients together to form a smooth, thick paste.

Patrick Perry

The Blue Crab, Norfolk

Stacey Haines

An authentic citizen of Tidewater, Chef Patrick Perry was born in Norfolk and has lived in Hampton Roads his entire life. Though Patrick's only professional chef experience has been at The Blue Crab, he grew up amid several restaurateurs. "When I was a child, I was seriously influenced by my uncle. He owned the Golden Pheasant Inn in Bucks County, Pennsylvania. His affinity for the culinary industry and his love of good food found its way into my life."

At The Blue Crab you'll find everyone in the family lending a hand. The quaint atmosphere and the view of Pretty Lake adds an unequivocal bonus to dining on fresh seafood and eclectic contemporary specials.

Chef Perry has received an enviable education working under local greats Monroe Duncan, Bobby Huber, and his own sister, Sherry Perry. These apprenticeships may be the key to the great success of The Blue Crab. Knowing what the Tidewater consumer likes and expects is a wisdom acquired from working with such prominent local chefs. To strengthen the money management aspect of his career, Chef Perry obtained a degree in finance from Old Dominion University.

Although he promotes democracy in the kitchen, Chef Perry understands that at certain moments there is no substitute for autocratic rule. "Things can heat up at times, especially in a small and open kitchen like ours. There is just no room for error on a plate." Another important part of Patrick's creed promotes sanitation and organization, noting that these two elements are crucial to the operation of his business.

At The Blue Crab, Chef Perry has the advantage of a beautiful atmosphere and view, and he recognizes that the food has to be just as good. "How disappointing it would be to sit in this restaurant, take in this beautiful view, and be served a less than superb product. I only serve the freshest ingredients and I always strive for consistency. I'm also here to make a living, so my ultimate responsibility is to maintain a profitable establishment."

A great example of a winner in the business, Chef Perry is testimony to the fact that self-made cooks can make it if they put their heart and soul into cooking. "The greatest advice that I can give is for people to use a good source and follow directions. Never rush through any part of the cooking process, and treat each step as importantly as the others. This is a no-fail way to master good cooking." Patrick experiences culinary enrichment everywhere he goes. This spirit helps him stay on top of the latest trends. "I

enjoy eating out and experiencing the great creations of our local chefs. We are very fortunate to have extremely talented chefs in the Tidewater area." While he admires chefs that exhibit a panache for theatrics, Chef Perry emphasizes that culinary education can be achieved anywhere and at anytime, as long as you look for it. "A chef's quest for perfection is literally shown on the plate that you ordered . . . what could be greater than that?"

The well-trained, personable wait staff and delicious, reasonably priced food keep the crowd at The Blue Crab coming back for more. "While you're at my restaurant, relax and have the best possible time you can. Also, don't be afraid to ask questions. It is easier for me to please you if I know what your desires are!"

Pepper-Crusted Seared Tuna with Wasabi Sauce

2 pounds thick-cut fresh tuna fillets, cut
    into 2" pieces
4 tablespoons whole black pepper
2 tablespoons vegetable oil

    Place plastic wrap over peppercorns and crush pepper with a mallet. Coat tuna with pepper.
    Heat oil over high temperature. Sear each side of tuna for approximately 30-45 seconds. Place tuna in refrigerator for 1 hour. With a razor sharp knife, cut tuna into paper thin slices. Serve cold with Wasabi Sauce on the side. **Serves 2**

Wasabi Sauce

1 tablespoon wasabi powder
cold water
⅓ cup soy sauce

    Mix the powder with enough water to make a paste. Cover with plastic wrap and set aside to develop flavor. After 10 minutes mix soy sauce and paste together until smooth.

Shrimp Danish Appetizer

2 ounces butter
2 tablespoons minced shallots
2 cups thinly sliced mushrooms
12 large shrimp, peeled and deveined
2 ounces brandy
½ cup Danish blue cheese

    In a small sauté pan add the butter, shallots, mushrooms and shrimp. Cook for about 1 minute over high heat. Add brandy and flambé. **(CAUTION: Remove pan from stove before adding brandy.)** When shrimp just turns opaque, add the blue cheese and toss lightly so the blue cheese does not melt. **Serves 2**

Oyster Stew

12 oysters in liquor
½ cup heavy whipping cream
1½ cups half & half
2 teaspoons butter
salt and white pepper to taste

    In a small pan combine all ingredients. Heat until the cream boils and the edges of oysters curl. **Serves 2**

Oyster Stuffing

½ teaspoon salt

½ teaspoon cayenne pepper

½ teaspoon garlic powder

½ teaspoon paprika

¼ teaspoon onion powder

¼ teaspoon dried oregano leaves

¼ teaspoon dried thyme leaves

30 small oysters in their liquor

1 cup chicken stock

6 ounces butter

1½ cups chopped onion

1 cup chopped celery

1 cup chopped green pepper

1 teaspoon minced garlic

1 (12 ounce) bag seasoned bread cubes

Preheat oven to 350°.

In a small mixing bowl, thoroughly combine all spices.

Drain liquor from oysters and set aside. Combine oysters with stock and refrigerate one hour. Drain the oysters and set this liquid aside.

In a large sauté pan combine the spice mixture, butter, onion, celery, green pepper, garlic and reserved oyster liquor and cook over medium temperature for about 6 minutes, stirring constantly.

In a medium mixing bowl, combine the bread crumbs and the cooked vegetable-spice mixture. Add the oysters, being careful not to break them. If dressing appears dry, add the reserved stock in ¼ cup increments until moist. Spoon dressing into an ungreased 9x12-inch baking pan and bake uncovered in oven for 30 minutes or until browned.

Crawfish and Andouille Omelet

1 link andouille sausage, sliced

3 eggs

½ cup heavy whipping cream

½ teaspoon Paul Prudhomme Seafood Magic

3 ounces crawfish tail meat

1 tablespoon butter

Preheat oven to 350°.

Brown sausage in a small sauté pan.

In a small mixing bowl, beat eggs. Set aside.

In a small sauté pan over high temperature add cream, Seafood Magic and crawfish. Reduce for approximately 2-4 minutes. Reserve cream and set aside.

Melt butter in omelet pan. Add beaten eggs to the pan. When the eggs are almost done add the sausage and crawfish. Bake in the oven 1-2 minutes. Remove from the oven and fold omelet onto plate. Pour the reserved cream sauce over the omelet and serve. **Serves 1**

Peter Pittman

Peter's Tentop/The Wild Monkey, Norfolk

Mealtime is a very important event for Chef Peter Pittman, and at Peter's Tentop and The Wild Monkey, you'll find out that the food takes center stage. Growing up as the youngest in a family of eight, there was always a lot of cooking to be done. Since his family members were born on opposite sides of the Mason-Dixon line, Chef Pittman knew about fusion cooking before its fashionable debut. "This arrangement created a peculiar culinary environment. Fusion of Northern and Southern cooking led to big meals and a lot of one-dish cookery." Having a big family also meant that there was a lot of preparation to be done. Peter learned at a young age how to peel, chop, and cook. "We all sat together at the same time every day to eat dinner." Chef Pittman admits that because of his hectic schedule he now rarely cooks at home, except for his favorite special occasions.

Coming from a history of nondescript, short-lived jobs, Chef Pittman is delighted to have found the restaurant industry to be as dynamic as it is. "With the different seasons, new trends, and the customers you meet, you never know what to expect." Showing his true passion, Chef Pittman finds it absolutely impossible to become bored with cooking. "There is so much experimenting you can do. Every time you try something, you can improve your product, and the world offers a constant learning experience. All of this makes for a very rewarding day."

Striving to represent his inner-self in his creations, Chef Pittman's food reflects his love for the great outdoors. He feels that an important part of cooking is taking the time to pair tastes, textures and colors on a plate. He also feels that it is imperative to consider the variety of vegetables and fruits available during each part of the year. "Everything that the season has to offer should be represented on your plate. At Peter's Tentop and The Wild Monkey, all of the bounties of the earth are represented on our seasonally changing menus."

Peter's lifestyle lends itself to a basic cooking style. "I let food do its own thing. Carrots taste like carrots, so learn how their flavors influence and complement other ingredients, or, just let a carrot be a carrot!" Chef Pittman's kitchen ethic proclaims that the less processing a food receives, the better. "I also believe meat and poultry cook and taste better with the bone in and the skin on."

Advice as easy as Chef Pittman's will help any cook gain more confidence and ability in the kitchen. "I feel that good cooking methods are more important than good recipes, that creativity is more important than knowledge, and that the end product justifies the means to obtaining it." According to Chef Pittman, there isn't a wrong way to cook anything as long as your meal looks good and tastes good, and you enjoyed making and eating it!

At Peter's Tentop, every employee is a craftsman in the kitchen. The hectic pace of a two-man kitchen requires employees to think on their feet and to remain cool under pressure. Open kitchens also require busy cooks to wear appealing smiles while they are getting down to serious business. "At our restaurants, you'll be greeted with a hearty 'hello' and a welcoming sensation. With an open kitchen, a customer sees their food being prepared, so they know its fresh, and that's what keeps people coming back."

Chef Pittman's newest restaurant, The Wild Monkey on Colley Avenue in Norfolk, will appeal to Peter's fans seeking sit-down dining served with the same smiles and pleasurable demeanor found at Ten Top. The Wild Monkey is a full-service restaurant where the diner-inspired menu reflects haute and fusion cuisines and everything is garnished with elán.

Molasses-Roasted Salmon Fillet

2 pound fresh salmon fillet, pin bones removed

1 tablespoon oil

2 tablespoons kosher salt

¼ cup blackstrap or old-fashioned molasses

2 tablespoons coarse ground pepper

Garnish: fresh herbs

    Preheat oven to 375°.

    Lay salmon, skin side down, on an oiled cookie sheet. With a sharp knife, score the salmon flesh ¼-inch deep in a criss-cross pattern, side to side, at about 1-inch intervals. Sprinkle the fish with kosher salt. Drizzle molasses onto the fish and rub into the cuts of the fillet with a wet hand. Coat the top of the salmon fillet evenly with pepper. Bake in oven for approximately 15 minutes. Let stand at room temperature for 5 minutes. Place on a heated platter and garnish with fresh herbs. **Serves 4**

Chef's Note: Don't ever be shy when it comes to buying fish. Always ask to smell your fish before you buy it. A reputable monger won't mind.

Spinach Feta Cakes

10 ounces fresh spinach

½ cup crumbled feta cheese

¼ cup low-fat mayonnaise

½ cup rehydrated sun-dried tomatoes

pinch of dry basil

2 eggs

¼ cup bread crumbs

    Rinse and dry spinach. Chop spinach, stems included, into thin ribbons. Do not overwork or process the spinach; leave it leafy and light.

    In a large mixing bowl with your hands, mix feta, mayonnaise, sun-dried tomatoes, basil and eggs. Add spinach. Sprinkle in bread crumbs and mix until smooth and bound. Let mixture stand while oven is preheating to 375°.

    Form mixture into four burger-like patties and bake for 16-20 minutes until firm and lightly browned. **Makes 4 cakes**

Chef's Note: We serve these cakes as a sandwich with a creamy dill dressing on an onion roll, but they make a great vegetarian entree as well.

Pan-Roasted Duck Breast in Bing Cabernet Sauce

1 tablespoon butter or olive oil

6 boneless duck breasts, skin on

3 cloves garlic, minced

1 tablespoon kosher salt

1 tablespoon coarse black pepper

Bing Cabernet Sauce (recipe to follow)

Preheat oven to 450°.

Place butter in an ovenproof skillet over medium-high temperature. Rub duck breasts with minced garlic, salt and pepper. Sauté breasts in a preheated skillet, skin side down for approximately 8 minutes. Flip breasts and roast in the skillet, in the oven, for 10. Remove from oven. Top with Bing Cabernet Sauce and serve. **Serves 6**

Bing Cabernet Sauce

1 bottle (750 ml) Cabernet Sauvignon

½ cup fresh chopped Bing cherries

½ cup well seasoned beef or lamb stock

⅓ cup honey

In a pan over medium-high temperature, simmer and reduce red wine by ⅔. Add cherries and stock and reduce by half. Add honey and reduce until syrup is thick and coats the back of a spoon. Keep warm.

Blue Ribbon Molasses Cookies

1 cup sugar (plus extra for rolling dough)

¾ cup vegetable shortening

½ cup unsulfered molasses

1 egg

2 cups all-purpose flour

1 teaspoon baking powder

1 teaspoon baking soda

1 teaspoon ground ginger

1 teaspoon cinnamon

½ teaspoon ground cloves

½ teaspoon nutmeg

¼ teaspoon salt

At medium speed, mix sugar and shortening with a hand mixer until smooth. Add molasses and egg and beat well.

In a separate bowl combine remaining ingredients. With mixer at low speed, add dry mixture to shortening mixture, beating until just blended. Wrap dough in plastic wrap and refrigerate a minimum of 2 hours.

Preheat oven to 375°.

Lightly grease cookie sheets. Form dough into 1-inch balls. Roll in extra sugar and place on cookie sheets approximately 2 inches apart. Bake 7-9 minutes. Remove from sheets and cool completely.

Chef's Note: These Blue Ribbon Molasses Cookies are truly award winning. My wife, Chris Watt Pittman won the Virginia State Fair cookie competition with this recipe.

Patrick Reed

Johnson & Wales University, Norfolk

Constantly in search of an outlet for his artistic passions, Chef Patrick Reed has turned to pastry! As a Chef Instructor at Johnson & Wales University, he understands his students need to express their artistic abilities. "We see our students getting younger all the time. Before, our Norfolk campus catered to an older crowd or those wanting a career change. Now we also have a large enrollment of people right out of high school. Many of them are musicians, artists, and theater people. I can draw a definite parallel between food and art. It's all about caring – about your craft and your audience."

Patrick was born and raised in Illion, New York, and has fond memories of a loving house filled with the aromas of bread baking and fresh coffee brewing. "This background has given me the basics needed to enjoy life. I'm hard working, thorough, and very organized, but I also love to relax and savor each day. Fortunately, my job is so enjoyable that I like it better than working!"

Chef Reed's first cooking experience was in the Navy. That's when he knew he wanted to be a chef. Even the hard-to-please sailors truly enjoyed his cooking. After leaving the Navy, he attended the Culinary Institute of America in Hyde Park, New York, for two years. In the Tidewater area, Patrick has worked as a pastry chef at the Chamberlain

Hotel, Monroe's Mocambo, and as a chef at Bella Monte. He also traveled to Hawaii and worked as a pastry chef at the Sunrise Bakery in Honolulu.

Other than cooking, Chef Reed's loves include reading, canoeing, camping, water sports, traveling, and music. An ex-musician, he has played big band, swing, jazz and orchestral music. His favorite avocation is eating out, and he likes to patronize establishments whose chefs have a flair for the dramatic. "The enjoyment has to begin when you walk in, and hopefully never end, thus becoming a good memory. You have to be able to relax and enjoy each segment of the meal, and you never want to be rushed. It takes some discipline to get to that point, to learn to slow down and enjoy food as a culinary delight."

Willing to travel anywhere at a moment's notice, Chef Reed pays attention to what is happening with food everywhere he goes. Being a pastry chef requires strict organization, but there is always room to be creative through experimentation or subtle twists. "It's challenging to improve or update a classic recipe – or to create a new food – but you can also get very creative with plate presentation, stacking and even fusion."

Chef Reed truly feels that culinary school graduates are a step ahead of beginning chefs,

but it is experience that makes the difference. "A culinary school education arms the student with the basics to call themselves a chef. They possess the tool . . . and they have the piece of paper to get in the door. After that it's up to them to build on their knowledge."

Johnson & Wales University has campuses in Providence, Rhode Island; Charleston, South Carolina; North Miami, Florida; Vail, Colorado; and Norfolk, Virginia. Johnson & Wales' success is attributed to its strong reputation and its progression into a fully accredited university with degrees in culinary, hospitality, and business concentrations. "The whole process of teaching is very gratifying." Chef Reed teaches several courses at Johnson & Wales University, but his first love is baking and pastry. This is where the true artist in him shines!

Meatloaf Roulade

1 pound lean ground beef

½ pound ground pork

½ pound ground veal

1 cup dry bread crumbs

3 eggs

¼ cup tomato paste

¼ cup chopped fresh cilantro

2 tablespoons chopped fresh basil

1 tablespoon finely chopped garlic

½ cup chopped onion

1 tablespoon PickaPeppa, A-1, Worcestershire
  Sauce, or barbecue sauce

1 teaspoon fresh ground black pepper

1 teaspoon salt

1½ cups Monterey Jack or white cheddar
  cheese, grated

jalapeños, stems removed, sliced thin, to taste

Preheat oven to 325°.

Combine all ingredients except cheese and jalapeños and mix well.

On a flat surface, lay out 2 sheets of film wrap or waxed paper to form an overlapping rectangle approximately 12x16-inches. Spread the mixture out in an even layer of equal thickness approximately, 10x14-inches. Sprinkle cheese over entire surface, leaving a ½-inch border at the sides to seal. Lay jalapeños in the center of the rectangle.

Roll the roulade toward you using the paper to keep the roll tight (as you would a jelly roll), removing the wrap as you roll. Seal the ends and the seam, keeping the seam on the bottom of the roll.

Transfer to a large roasting pan and bake, uncovered for approximately 1 hour and 20 minutes, or to an internal temperature of 140°. **Serves 8**

Orange and Cranberry Quick Bread

2 ounces butter

1 cup sugar

1 large egg

zest of 1 orange

2 cups cake flour

1 cup whole wheat flour

2 teaspoons baking powder

1 teaspoon baking soda

½ cup fresh wheat germ

1 teaspoon kosher salt

2 cups whole canned cranberries in sauce

juice of 1 orange

Preheat oven to 350°.

Cream butter and sugar until light and fluffy. Blend egg and orange zest together thoroughly, and add to butter and sugar mixture. Combine flours, baking powder, baking soda, wheat germ and salt.

Drain cranberries, reserving the juice. Combine the cranberry juice with the orange juice and add to the butter and sugar mixture.

Alternately, add the dry and wet ingredients together in a bowl, and thoroughly mix. Gently fold in cranberries and pour into a greased and floured 9x5x3-inch loaf pan. Bake for approximately 1 hour. **Makes 1 loaf**

Chef's Note: For best results, freeze the cranberries and toss them with 1 tablespoon of flour before folding into batter.

Fast Vegetarian Chili

2 tablespoons + 1 teaspoon cumin seed

2 tablespoons dry oregano

6-8 tablespoons pure olive oil

3 cups chopped onion

2 cups chopped red pepper

1½ tablespoons minced garlic

1 tablespoon salt

2 tablespoons paprika

1 teaspoon cayenne pepper

1 teaspoon fresh ground black pepper

1 (28 ounce) can crushed tomatoes

3-6 tablespoons chopped jalapeños

1 (15 ounce) can black beans, drained,
    juices reserved

1 (15 ounce) can kidney beans, drained,
    juices reserved

1 (15 ounce) can garbanzo beans, drained,
    juices reserved

1 (15 ounce) can white beans, drained,
    juices reserved

3 tablespoons cornmeal, as needed

In a large, deep, heavy bottomed saucepot heat all cumin seed and oregano over medium temperature for about 3 minutes.

Add olive oil, onion, red peppers, garlic, salt, paprika, cayenne and black pepper and cook approximately 10-15 minutes, or until vegetables are tender.

Add crushed tomatoes, jalapeños, beans and enough reserved bean juice to just cover the mixture. Simmer at least 20 minutes to blend flavors. **Serves 8**

Chef's Note: If the mixture is too soupy, stir in cornmeal 1 tablespoon at a time over simmering chili at 5 minute intervals until desired thickness is achieved.

Patrick's Cabbage Pie

pastry crust for a 9" pie (double crust, deep dish)

½ cup good quality olive oil

1 head (5 cups) white cabbage, shredded

1 large onion, sliced lengthwise, same size as shredded cabbage

½ teaspoon dry basil

½ teaspoon dry oregano

½ teaspoon dry tarragon

salt and pepper to taste

1½ cups sliced mushrooms

3 ounces cream cheese

4 hard boiled eggs, sliced

1 tablespoon fresh dill, chopped

Preheat oven to 350°.

In a large open sauté pan, heat ¼ cup of the olive oil and sauté the cabbage, onion, and herbs over medium temperature stirring frequently so the juices evaporate and the cabbage and onion are very soft, approximately 25 minutes. While cabbage is cooking, sauté mushrooms in remainder of olive oil until softened, approximately 5-8 minutes.

To assemble, line a deep dish pie tin with crust. Spread cream cheese over crust. Lay egg slices in a single layer on top of the cream cheese and sprinkle with dill. Pile in cabbage mixture and mushrooms. Top with pastry, seal, vent, and bake for 45 minutes until deep golden brown. **Serves 4 as a Main Dish, 8 as a Side Dish**

Peanut Butter and Chocolate Mousse Pie

2 (9") graham cracker crusts

Peanut Butter Mousse

12 ounces cream cheese

1 cup smooth peanut butter

1 cup sugar

1 cup heavy whipping cream

1½ teaspoons vanilla

Blend cream cheese, peanut butter and sugar on medium speed until very light, fluffy and smooth. Whip cream and vanilla into stiff peaks. Fold carefully into peanut butter mixture.

Chocolate Mousse

8 ounces bittersweet chocolate, fine chop

1 egg

2 egg yolks

2 egg whites, whipped to stiff peaks

½ cup heavy cream, whipped to stiff peaks

Over a double boiler, melt chocolate halfway. Take off heat and stir to melt completely. Combine whole egg and egg yolks in a separate double boiler. Whip over low temperature until lemony colored and you see the volume expanding.

Off heat, quickly combine warm chocolate with warm egg mixture, stirring to cool to room temperature. Carefully fold in whipped egg whites and whipped cream, ensuring there are no white streaks.

Preheat oven to 350°.

Completely line a 10x3-inch springform pan with graham cracker crust and bake for 5-8 minutes to set.

After crust has cooled, pile in peanut butter mousse so it fills pan halfway. Freeze to firm slightly, about 30 minutes.

Pile in chocolate mousse to top of pan, and chill pie a minimum of 3 hours before slicing. **Serves 12**

Chef's Note: This pie freezes well, and in fact comes out of the pan and slices better if partially frozen. The chocolate and peanut butter combination always works. A nice garnish is a rosette of whipped cream with a miniature peanut butter cup candy on each slice. It is a hint of what's inside!

Brie, Sage and Garlic Bread

1 teaspoon sugar

1½ cups warm water

1 package active dry yeast

3½ cups bread flour

2 teaspoons salt

4 tablespoons roasted garlic, mashed
    and puréed

2 tablespoons fresh sage, rough chop

6 grindings black pepper

3 ounces Brie cheese, shredded

egg wash

salt

Combine sugar and water. Sprinkle yeast over top to dissolve. Cover and set in a warm place for 5-7 minutes or until the yeast begins to foam well.

Combine 3 cups of flour, salt, garlic, sage and freshly ground pepper. Blend thoroughly. Add yeast mixture and knead to a smooth soft dough, adding extra flour as needed to make the dough elastic but not sticky. (This process should take 8-10 minutes by hand to properly develop the dough.)

Place dough in a lightly oiled large bowl, rolling dough so that oil seals the surface of the dough from the dry air, then cover with plastic wrap. Set in a warm place and let rise until double (approximately 1 hour, ½ hour if using dry instant yeast).

Punch down dough to expel the excess CO_2 and reform dough into a smooth ball. Massage in Brie. Cover with inverted bowl and let the dough relax 10 minutes to become manageable.

Preheat oven to 350°.

Shape dough into individual rolls or one loaf. Place formed rolls on a sheet pan dusted with cornmeal. If making a loaf, grease a loaf pan and lightly dust with cornmeal. Lightly cover with plastic and let rise in a warm spot until double. When almost double in size, gently brush with egg wash that includes a sprinkle of salt.

Bake until deep golden brown and hollow sounding when tapped.

Chef's Note: It helps to freeze the Brie until almost solid for easy shredding. If you prefer to substitute another cheese, a good choice would be Gruyère or Emmentaler.

Hans Schadler

The Williamsburg Inn, Williamsburg

Ever since he was a boy, Hans Schadler has been actively involved in all aspects of food preparation. At the age of ten, Hans had daily tasks preparing food for his family and shyly admits that he was more interested in the machinery of cooking than cooking itself. His father nudged him toward a culinary career and brought him to the Savoy Hotel and Opera Restaurant in Frankfurt, Germany. "That was hard work! There was sawdust on the floors, wood-burning ovens, hand-pull dumb waiters and limited refrigeration. I also worked for a very disciplined escoffier chef, so it goes without saying that I learned a lot. European schools focus on the fundamentals of culinary arts and work at making you a good cook, while additional training and knowledge is continuous throughout your career."

After receiving his degree, Hans worked in every brigade position at various hotels and resorts in Germany, Switzerland and Norway. He then worked for the Norwegian-American Line on a five year cruise that took him around the world. "My biggest objective was to work for a quality organization, so I used this opportunity to establish myself as a professional." His next adventure took him to the U.S. Virgin Islands, where he joined Rockresort's Caneel Bay Plantation as a sous chef, later being promoted to Executive Chef. In 1982, at the peak of his career, Hans Schadler made his way to

Williamsburg, Virginia. "My family and I came to see the property, and I knew in my heart that there was a good future for us here. The Williamsburg Inn is a quality-driven organization, and that means everything to me." In 1988, Hans was selected by Nancy Reagan as her first-choice replacement for departing White House chef Henry Haller. He did not accept this position due to his commitment and loyalty to his home, Colonial Williamsburg.

There just aren't enough hours in a day for Hans Schadler to accomplish everything he wishes to do. Today's chef has to wear many hats. "The human aspect of the job is very important to me, yet I realize that you can't be everything to everyone. That only leads to disappointment." Hans works very hard at trying to set an example, and he helps build career paths for all of his employees. "You have a feeling when they are ready to move on to the next level."

Chef Schadler firmly believes that the United States is one of the top culinary nations in the world. "Every nationality that has come here has added to this great blending and people should really take advantage of this." At The Williamsburg Inn, a great deal of thought is put into its classical ambience. The menu is designed to take full advantage of the Tidewater region and its seasons.

With everyone taking entertaining and

cooking more seriously than ever, the home cook can learn a great deal from the commercial chef's practices and advice. "You must have the desire to want to shine in front of people. This can easily be achieved if you know your parameters, select entrees with your capability in mind, get a plan together, and do what you can ahead of time." You should always bring quality and expert touches to your table. "A simple garnish can make a big difference."

At The Williamsburg Inn, you will undoubtedly walk away from your dining experience satisfied with all phases of your meal. "I take a lot of pride in serving food at its correct temperature. This is probably one of the most important aspects of presentation. If there is an architectural design on your plate, it probably took a long time to do, and the quality of the food becomes compromised." Hans is a firm believer in every item on a plate having a meaning, and he wants his diners to find pleasure in them all. "We tend to serve a traditional clientele here, but sometimes I get surprised. People are becoming more adventurous, and I like that."

Virginia Ham Pâté

1 pound Virginia ham

2 cups mayonnaise

2 tablespoons Dijon mustard

3 ounces Nut Chutney (recipe to follow)

Grind ham very fine. Mix ham together with remaining ingredients to a spreadable consistency. **Serves 8**

Nut Chutney

1 cup water

½ cup distilled white vinegar

½ cup sugar

arrowroot or cornstarch for thickening

½ cup chopped cashews

½ cup chopped pecans

½ cup chopped almonds

½ cup chopped filberts

½ cup chopped Brazils

½ cup chopped pistachios

1 cup mango or papaya, small dice

1 cup ginger, fresh or candied, small dice

1 green pepper, small dice

1 red pepper, small dice

1 yellow pepper, small dice

¼ cup chopped parsley or fresh chives

In a saucepan, combine water, vinegar and sugar. Over low temperature, let cook for approximately 30 minutes. Thicken with arrowroot. Let cool.

Place remaining ingredients into a large mixing bowl. Add sugar base and mix well. May be kept refrigerated for 2-5 days.

Chef's Note: If mango or papaya is out of season, substitute with cantaloupe. For a quick version, purchase a jar of Major Grey Chutney and add nuts listed above.

Crème Brûlée

1 cup milk

1 cup heavy cream

⅔ cup sugar

1 vanilla bean, split

4 egg yolks

Preheat oven to 300°.

In a heavy saucepan heat milk, heavy cream, sugar and vanilla bean. Bring to a boil and immediately remove from heat. Strain through a fine sieve.

In a medium-size bowl, beat egg yolks. Slowly add the cream mixture to the egg yolks and mix thoroughly.

Place mixture into buttered ramekins and bake for approximately 45 minutes or until almost firm to the touch. Allow to cool. Refrigerate until needed.

To serve, generously cover with granulated sugar and quickly broil or torch until sugar begins to caramelize. **Serves 6**

Horseradish Mousse

1½ pounds cream cheese

1 cup prepared horseradish

1 cup sour cream

lemon juice to taste

cayenne pepper to taste

3½ ounces plain gelatin granules

2 cups hot water

1 cup lightly whipped cream

In a large mixing bowl, combine the first 5 ingredients.

In a separate bowl, mix gelatin and hot water together. Stir until gelatin dissolves. Add gelatin mixture to cream cheese mixture. Gently fold in whipped cream.

Lay mixture out on a piece of plastic wrap and roll into a log. Refrigerate until set, approximately 4 hours.

To serve, slice off portions from the log. **Serves 8**

Chef's Note: This is an excellent accompaniment to smoked seafood and meats.

Pecan Pie

pastry crust for a 9" pie

4 eggs

¾ cup sugar

½ teaspoon salt

1½ cups light corn syrup

1 tablespoon butter, melted and cooled

1 teaspoon vanilla

1 cup pecan halves

Preheat oven to 400°.

Prepare crust and line a 9-inch pie pan with dough.

Beat eggs lightly and add sugar, salt, corn syrup, butter and vanilla. Stir until well mixed.

Spread the pecan halves on pie crust. Pour filling on top of pecans. Place in oven and immediately reduce heat to 350°. Bake 40-50 minutes or until the pie is firm in the center. Cool before serving. **Serves 8**

Sautéed Soft-Shell Crabs

juice of 1 lemon

1 tablespoon Worcestershire Sauce

8 medium soft-shell crabs, cleaned

2 cups egg wash

½ cup sifted flour

½ cup yellow cornmeal

1 cup unsalted clarified butter

In a medium-size bowl, mix lemon juice and Worcestershire together.

Marinate crabs in mixture for 30 minutes. Dip in egg wash, flour and then cornmeal. Shake off excess cornmeal. Heat a large skillet over medium-high temperature. Add clarified butter and heat until hot. Sauté crabs 1 minute on each side. **Serves 4**

Chef's Note: An excellent sauce for this dish is a modified béarnaise sauce. Start with a basic béarnaise sauce and add Dijon mustard, Tabasco Sauce, peeled minced tomato and puréed watercress. Mix well and serve over crabs.

Warm Spring Salad of Seafood and Garden Mix with Plum Tomato-Basil Vinaigrette and Goat Cheese

Seafood Marinade (recipe to follow)

Garden Mix (recipe to follow)

Plum Tomato-Basil Vinaigrette (recipe to follow)

¼ cup olive oil

6 ounces mixed seafood (shrimp, scallops, lobster,
  flounder or any other firm fish)

1 shallot, minced

1 clove garlic, minced

1 medium zucchini, sliced

1 teaspoon herbes de Provençe

salt and pepper to taste

1 medium ripe tomato, sliced, chilled

2 ounces goat cheese, crumbled

Garnish: fresh basil leaves and fresh crusty bread

Heat olive oil in a non-stick skillet or wok. Sear marinated seafood to ensure that all pieces are well caramelized and done, but do not overcook. Remove from pan. Set aside and keep warm.

Add shallot and garlic to the pan. Sauté, but do not brown. Add zucchini and herbs. Sauté for approximately 1 minute. Season to taste with salt and pepper. Remove from heat and keep warm.

To assemble, arrange warm zucchini and chilled tomato in a ring around a plate.

Carefully arrange Garden Mix in center of the ring. Garnish Mix with seafood. Drizzle with vinaigrette and top with crumbled cheese. Garnish with fresh basil leaves and serve with fresh crusty bread. Repeat for second serving.

Serves 2

Seafood Marinade

2 teaspoons chopped fresh dill

2 teaspoons chopped fresh thyme

1 tablespoon chopped fresh parsley

salt and fresh cracked pepper

1 garlic clove, mashed

¼ -½ cup olive oil

Mix ingredients together. Pour over seafood and chill for 30-45 minutes.

Garden Mix

1 medium ripe tomato, sliced, chilled

1 cup assorted salad greens

3 red radishes, sliced and cut in strips

2 tablespoons red wine vinegar

2 tablespoons olive oil

salt and pepper to taste

In a stainless steel bowl, toss greens and radishes with oil and vinegar. Season with salt and pepper.

(continued on next page)

Plum Tomato-Basil Vinaigrette

¼ *cup olive oil*

1 garlic clove, crushed

2 medium shallots, minced

2 ripe Italian plum tomatoes, peeled,
    seeded and diced

1 tablespoon fresh basil, chopped

1 green onion, fine dice

1 tablespoon fresh lime juice

2 tablespoons red wine vinegar

salt and fresh ground black pepper to taste

    Using the same skillet used to sear seafood, lightly heat olive oil. Add garlic and shallots and sweat lightly. Add tomatoes, basil and onion and toss well. Add lime juice and vinegar. Season with salt and pepper. Shake well.

David Watts

Cafe David, VA Beach

Chef David Watts offers a varied and exciting cuisine on his new menu at Cafe David. He hopes the new name of his restaurant (formerly Bella Pasta) will let people know that Italian isn't the only food offered. "We changed the name because it stifled my range of creativity. Now we offer a mixed cuisine, which is what I really love to cook. Cross-cultural cuisine can be very interesting."

Chef Watts is a native of Norfolk, Virginia. At sixteen he went to Vermont to work for his brother's rock band. Eight years later David's interest in food preparation began. "When the band broke up, I needed a job. I was washing dishes in a restaurant, and one day the lunch chef didn't show up. The owner asked me to fill in, and that is where I began as a chef." David worked as a chef in various locations for ten years before he studied at The New England Culinary Institute. "I was learning a lot working under different chefs, but people want to see that culinary diploma – even though a culinary graduate may not have any practical experience." Before returning to Norfolk, Chef Watts worked for both independent and corporate chain restaurants in New England. "Working within corporate guidelines was a new experience for me. You are trained in a very specific manner and the key element is speed. You have to do things quickly and correctly."

David's love for cooking comes from his mother. "She is from Naples, Italy. She used to cook such grand meals – and the kitchen would be a mess! The passion she added to her cooking really made things taste great." David's wife, Pamela, is also a wonderful southern cook, and her influences are seen at Cafe David. Constantly searching for new ideas, Chef Watts doesn't even stop working while on vacation. Like many chefs, his vacations center around food and dining out, but David takes it a step further: "As we travel on our vacations, I eat out every chance I get, and I collect menus. When I find a really great place, I ask if I can work in the kitchen. I promise not to get in their way, and I'll even wash dishes for a few hours just to be able to watch a talented chef at work."

Developing new dishes can be very challenging for the independent chef. "There really isn't anything new under the sun. You have to constantly read food magazines, follow the food trends, and give foods a new twist. At the same time, you have to keep things as simple as possible while using the best ingredients available."

The success of Cafe David and Chef Watts is fed by word of mouth, but sometimes he is frustrated by that fact. "I think we have a reputation among other chefs and restaurants as a good place to eat. It's very hard for an independent restaurant to get that message to a broad range of the population. Certain restaurants always seem to get notoriety, and it can be frustrating when restaurants that aren't that good are always crowded, and good restaurants sometimes struggle. We need to educate the Tidewater population about food and what real dining is all about."

Chef Watts is influenced by the traditional, world-renowned chefs who use the methods they grew up with and hold taste above all else. "That's where you get your basic knowledge from. Everything needs to be done in moderation, but some foods just don't taste good without salt or butter."

Cafe David's current menu is a combination of the new and the old. Many of the latest dishes were incorporated from "specialty board" items that became popular favorites. "We are still going to have Bella Pasta favorites on the menu. It's never a problem to get whatever you want. If I have the ingredients and the ability, I'll cook it for you."

Red Pepper and Corn Soup

4 cloves garlic, roasted

1¾ cup fresh corn kernels

3 cups chicken stock

1 cup chopped onions

½ cup chopped carrots

½ cup chopped celery

1 jalapeño, seeded and chopped

2 cups heavy cream

3 red bell peppers, roasted and peeled

¼ teaspoon cayenne pepper

salt

Red Pepper Soup

In a medium saucepan over high temperature, combine roasted peppers, 1½ cups chicken stock, ½ cup chopped onion, ¼ cup carrots, ¼ cup celery and cayenne pepper. Bring to a boil. Reduce temperature and simmer 10 minutes.

Transfer Red Pepper Soup to a blender and purée. Strain through a fine sieve back into the saucepan. Add 1 cup heavy cream and simmer until thickened, about 5 minutes. Season to taste with salt.

Corn Soup

In another medium saucepan over high temperature, combine roasted garlic, corn, 1½ cups chicken stock, ½ cup chopped onion, ¼ cup carrots, ¼ cup celery and jalapeño. Bring to a boil. Reduce temperature and simmer for 10 minutes.

Transfer Corn Soup to a blender and purée thoroughly. Strain through a fine sieve back into the saucepan. Add 1 cup heavy cream and simmer until thickened, about 5 minutes. Season to taste with salt. Set aside and keep warm.

To serve each, gently reheat both soups in their separate saucepans. With 2 ladles, slowly and simultaneously ladle soups into one warm bowl. **Serves 4**

 # Tuna Havana

⅓ cup lime juice

1 cup peanut oil

1 tablespoon cracked black pepper

1 large red onion, julienne

4 (6 ounce) tuna steaks

Preheat grill.

In a mixing bowl, combine lime juice, oil, pepper and red onion. Marinate tuna in oil mixture for 10 minutes. Reserve marinade, separating onions for later use.

Grill tuna for 3-5 minutes on each side, or until done.

In a skillet, heat ½ cup of the reserved marinade. Add all of the reserved onions and reheat thoroughly. (Discard any unused marinade). Top the grilled tuna with the onions and drizzle with the hot marinade. **Serves 4**

Appetizer of Pan-Seared Scallops

1 tablespoon oil

1 pound sea scallops

salt and pepper to taste

1 pound mixed salad greens

½ cup cashews

1 red bell pepper, julienne

Vinaigrette Dressing (recipe to follow)

Prepare Vinaigrette Dressing and set aside.

In a large skillet heat oil. Season scallops with salt and pepper. Sear for 1-2 minutes on each side. Remove from skillet.

Divide salad greens onto 4 plates. Divide scallops into 4 portions and place on top of salad greens. Drizzle salads with vinaigrette dressing. Garnish each salad with cashews and red pepper strips. **Serves 4**

Vinaigrette Dressing

⅓ cup red wine vinegar

½ teaspoon salt

½ teaspoon white pepper

1 teaspoon curry powder

1 teaspoon Dijon mustard

1 cup oil

In a mixing bowl, add vinegar, salt, white pepper, curry powder and mustard. With a mixer on medium, beat to mix thoroughly. With mixer beating, slowly add oil, incorporating well.

Bananas Flambé

2 ounces butter

½ cup brown sugar

2 bananas, peeled, cut lengthwise

1 ounce dark rum

1 ounce banana liqueur

¼ cup walnuts, broken

4 bowls vanilla ice cream

In a skillet over medium temperature, melt butter. Add brown sugar, stirring continuously until it dissolves.

Add bananas to the sugar and butter mixture.

Remove from heat and quickly add rum and banana liqueur. Return to heat. (**CAUTION:** alcohol may flame when returned to the heat.) Add walnuts.

Divide evenly over ice cream and serve immediately.

Serves 4

Culinary Artists Index